FOR KEEPS

Meaningful Patchwork for Everyday Living

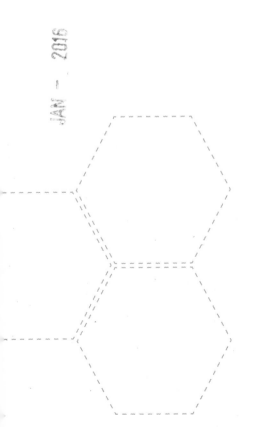

AMY GIBSON

Published in 2015 by Lucky Spool Media, LLC
www.luckyspool.com
info@luckyspool.com

Text © Amy Gibson
Editor Susanne Woods
Designer Liz Quan
Illustrations Kari Vojtechovsky
Photographer © John S. Miller, except where noted

The information in this book is accurate and complete to the best of our knowledge. All recommendations are made without guarantee on the part of the author or Lucky Spool Media, LLC. The author and publisher disclaim any liability in connection with this information.

Photographs pages 11-15, 17, 19-23, 25, 27-38, 40, 41, 43, 44, 49, 51, 52, 61, 66, 78, 81, 83, 85, 89, 93, 98, 104, 107, 109, 111, 114, 115, 120, 131 © Amy Gibson

Photographs pages 82, 88, 92, 93 © Erin Cox Photography

9 8 7 6 5 4 3 2 1

First Edition
Printed in USA

Library of Congress Cataloging-in-Publication Data available upon request

ISBN 978-1-940655-07-9

LSID0022

DEDICATION

To the One who put this passion in my heart
in the first place: thank you for sending me on this
trajectory and for lighting my path along the way.
And to my husband, Russell, and my four precious babies:
you are my joy, my laughter, my safe place.
Thank you for your ceaseless inspiration and
support, and for all the sacrifices you made
so this book could happen.

ACKNOWLEDGEMENTS

I'm so incredibly grateful to: Susanne Woods for taking a chance on me and believing in my vision. Liz Quan and Kari Vojtechovsky for bringing this book to life with such amazing design work. Shea Henderson and Lisa Lester for the editing that made sense of it all. John S. Miller for the beautiful photos that capture the heart of this project. Windham Fabrics for providing oodles of gorgeous material to work with. Cherry Creek Valley Historical Society for allowing me to photograph in the wonderful Melvin Schoolhouse. All the talented quilters who shared their time and talents with me: Karen O'Connor, Lyn Burg, Helen Burg, Sally Squire, Susan Santistevan, Linda Barrett and Amy Wade.

Dear friends (you know who you are), who showered me with encouragement and moral support from day one. Thank you for letting this crazy lady bombard your phone with top-secret quilt pictures!

And to my Mom and Dad: I can't begin to put my thanks into words … for your nurturing, your love, your support, for all the babysitting; all the brainstorming, the editing, the planning, for the late-night prayers and early-morning photo shoots. Thank you from the bottom of my heart.

CONTENTS

INTRODUCTION

Quilting for Keeps

To me, making a quilt to be an heirloom is like giving yourself a nickname. It feels forced, and it rarely ends up meaning quite what we want it to mean. Most of us have a quilt, or a stack of old quilts, hidden away in a chest or closet—gorgeous, hand-stitched masterpieces that carry priceless sentimentality because of their history, quilts that padded the seat of the covered wagon that brought our ancestors west, or hung to dry from the clothesline behind Mom and Dad's old farmhouse. You may be reading this book because you're hoping to create some treasures

yourself — knowing that quilts can be, and often are, so very much more than a pretty blanket.

I believe that a quilt, or any item, becomes memorable not simply because it exists, but because it carries with it something worth remembering. Quilts speak to us. They comfort and warm us, inside and out. They welcome us, and they send us off. They celebrate and grieve with us, and more than anything, they connect us with each other. And that's what I hope to spark through this book: the making of quilts that soak up meaning through our times together;

that become heirlooms — not just because of their ancestry and meticulous construction, or because of their designer fabrics and bold piecing—but because of the stories they tell and the stories they inspire.

When you stitch a quilt, it's difficult not to pour your heart into it. We can't help but dream about the perfect pattern; we agonize over fabric selection; we prick our fingers and rip out seams — all to make sure it turns out just right. My goal for this book is to take that passion for patchwork— my passion and I hope yours — and nudge it to the next level, to that intangible place where we go beyond quality construction, to craft our quilts in such a way that we employ them into our lives, making them not only for their aesthetic value but to be a part of the intentional strengthening of what life is all about: meaningful relationships.

This book is divided into three sections: A Patchwork Primer, Memory Maker projects, and Memory Keeper projects.

A Patchwork Primer

The first section dives into basic patchwork and quilting techniques, including loads of tips and ideas on tools and materials, piecing and finishing basics, high-efficiency quilting strategies, and design inspiration.

Memory Makers

Projects in this section are intended to encourage deliberate ways in which new stories could be written and memories made. The Popped quilt gives movie night an extra dash of fun, and the Once Upon a Time pocket pillow encourages reading together. These chapters share stories and offer ideas for quality time with the ones you love.

Memory Keepers

Other projects in the book fall into the Memory Keeper category. These are projects rooted in preserving memories of times gone by, and infusing them with more longevity and everyday use. The Filmstrip quilt is a way to bring photos out of our devices and into our homes. The Love Letters quilt honors the ever-personal handwritten word, and the Family Secrets recipe binder honors those beloved family dishes

that have earned a spot in our traditions. These chapters are meant to encourage the use of patchwork as a way of capturing and honoring meaningful stories and traditions.

I offer instructions on making the projects in this book the way that I made them, but I strongly encourage you to make adjustments to fit your own preferences. After all, the projects you create will be yours, not mine! I want you to love them, and I want you to love making them. Maybe you don't want to use two squares each of 18 prints for your recipe binder—maybe you want to use 32 different prints. Do it! For your Stargazer quilt, maybe you prefer a light background instead of dark. Do it! Perhaps you prefer to make your half-square triangles differently, or you enjoy hand appliqué more than by machine. Or you might want a larger quilt —add blocks, add borders, add dashing. Please, please promise me you'll personalize these projects to suit your tastes, skills, and preferences.

I believe that the art of patchwork really boils down to two foundation things: the final product, and equally important, how you got there. It's not about how closely you followed the pattern or matched the author's choices. It's about doing something that you love to do, making things that you love to make, and creating keepsakes that speak your heart and bring joy to yourself and those around you. If this book offers you anything, I hope that it's the inspiration to intentionally infuse your quilting with even more meaning, even more joy, even more intention, even more creativity.

Both the Memory Makers and the Memory Keepers are deeply rooted in intention, but I realize that these projects may not carry the same meaning or intention for you or your family. The Make Your Move game board quilt could spark a lively game of checkers, yes, or it could simply be a great quilt to take a nap under — the choice is completely up to you. I don't want you to feel limited by the unique way in which my family enjoys these pieces. Quilts are quilts, and there are so many fabulous ways to enjoy them. I hope that you will make these projects, not necessarily with my intentions behind them, but — and this is the crux — simply with an intention, whatever that may be for you. Make quilts you love, for people you love, to use every day.

Quilt for keeps.

A PATCHWORK PRIMER

QUILT MAKING BASICS FROM A TO Z

Every great keepsake quilt starts with solid construction. In this section, I will show you everything you need to know to get started making quilts that will not only look beautiful and stand the test of time for future generations, but—let's be real —will survive today's tepee, catnap, and super-hero flight.

If you already have a strong grasp of these basics, feel free to skip ahead, but don't miss the One-Woman Factory chapter coming up next, where I share a bit of family history and some tips and techniques to help you get more patchwork done in less time. After that, be sure to check out A Color Is Worth a Thousand Words, where I offer strategies for inspired fabric selection.

So, are you ready to quilt? Let's get started!

Choosing the Right Sewing Machine for You

First things first: you'll need a basic sewing machine that has a nice straight stitch, as well as an adjustable zigzag stitch. Some form of blind stitch or blanket stitch will also come in handy (for machine appliqué). Additional decorative stitches can seem like an exciting feature, but when it comes to quilting purposes, you will rarely, if ever, use them; so keep that in mind as you scope out machines. If you plan to try your hand at free-motion quilting (it's so much fun!), be sure your machine's feed dogs can be lowered. No other fancy features are required to get the job done, though some quilters enjoy the convenience of a needle threader, an automatic thread cutter, and automatic needle-down position.

Image courtesy of Craftsy (www.craftsy.com)

A few sewing machine shopping tips

𝐼 Be sure you can try the machine out before you buy it, and make sure you're aware of any warranties or return policies. If the machine is used, ask when and where it was last serviced.

𝐼 Read online reviews to get an idea of other quilters' experiences on the model you're considering.

𝐼 Find out what kind of technical support and customer service is offered by the manufacturer and if replacement parts are still available. Keep in mind that eBay and other online retailers offer a nearly unlimited source for discontinued or vintage sewing machine parts.

"Helen," my little Featherweight friend.

𝐼 Is the machine computerized, or are the workings strictly mechanical? Personally, I am less inclined toward computerized options and tend to favor a more mechanical machine with as much metal as humanly possible, not only for the durability but also because I enjoy a heavier weight machine that doesn't bounce around when I stitch at high speeds. Test a variety of types of machines to find out what your preferences are.

𝐼 If you plan to bring your machine to quilt guild meetings, classes, or conferences, portability is another factor to keep in mind. Some machines come with hard, protective covers and carrying handles, and others do not. I love toting my little Singer Featherweight around whenever I travel!

𝐼 If you're new to sewing, keep in mind that your very first machine need not be your "ultimate" machine, nor is it likely to be. The more you sew, the more you'll discover what features you prefer, and which you could do without.

Tools and Supplies

Now that you have your machine, let's gather the basic quilt making tools and supplies you'll need to get started.

PRESSER FEET

There are a few different types of presser feet needed for piecing and quilting, and these may or may not be included with your particular machine. A ¼" or "patchwork" foot works wonderfully for accurate piecing (I rarely take mine off), and a walking foot and darning foot are essential for machine quilting.

Presser feet essentials: ¼" patchwork foot, walking foot with guide, and darning foot.

SELF-HEALING CUTTING MATS

The larger the mat you can get (which fits into your space), the better. I recommend at least an 18" x 24", and if you can go larger, do it. It's so helpful to be able to spread out your materials, and not have to worry about constantly folding and rearranging larger pieces of fabric to fit on the mat surface. Take care to store your mat in a flat position (not standing or leaning), as it can warp in these positions over time. Also, keep all heat sources away from your mat, including your iron, laptop, or hot mugs or plates; heat can permanently warp and distort the mat.

ROTARY CUTTERS

Rotary cutters are available in a variety of sizes. A 45mm blade is the standard for most cutting, while a 28mm blade is great for smaller patches or curves. I actually enjoy using my 28mm cutter for much of my basic cutting because it offers added control and maneuverability. A large 60mm cutter works well for trimming thicker layers, such as squaring up your finished quilt.

TIP

For best results, change your rotary cutter blade often. How will you know when? If you start having to make more than one pass to get a single smooth cut, it's time for a new blade.

RULERS

Clear acrylic quilting rulers come in a wide variety of shapes and sizes. The most basic rulers to start with are the 6½" x 24", which is perfect for cutting strips of yardage (fabric cut straight from a bolt); as well as the 12½", 9½", and 4½" squares, which are very common block sizes. You could use a larger ruler, such as the 12½" square, to trim most all block sizes. The added convenience of being able to center a ruler on a block and trim all around it at once, without having to reposition may be worth the added cost of purchasing multiple rulers. Be sure your square rulers have at least one 45 degree (diagonal) marking, as well as ¼" markings along at least two of the edges.

TIP

If your rulers don't come with a non-slip underside, consider adding a product specifically designed to give the bottom of your quilting rulers more grip, preventing slippage while you cut. I like Invisi-Grip by Omnigrid, which acts like a window cling, but there are other great new product options popping up all the time, so search online or ask at your local quilt shop for recommendations.

STRAIGHT PINS

I prefer the flat flower head pins because they're easy to grasp and they lie flat on the fabric, minimizing any puckering or bumps. They're also long and slender, slipping in and out of the fabric easily without leaving any holes. As if you need any more reason to love these pretty pins, you can iron over them without melting the heads. Love 'em!

GLUE

Glue can be used in various ways throughout the piecing process. Gluing seams with Elmer's school glue and thin glue bottle tips has become a popular option to use in place of pinning for several reasons. It offers a more secure alignment with no chance of fabric shifting, and can make stitching faster and more relaxing as there are no pins to pull out. I also like this option because —as a mom of little ones — it's great to be able to leave out a stack of patches ready to be stitched and know that curious little fingers won't be poked, or pull out all my carefully placed pins.

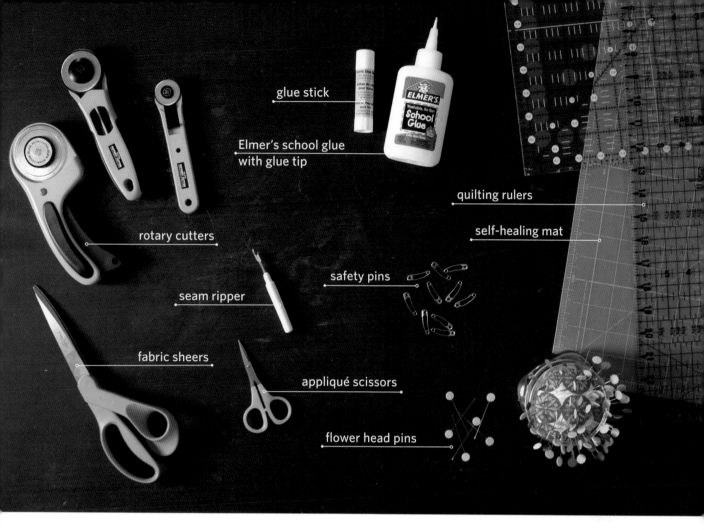

glue stick

Elmer's school glue
with glue tip

rotary cutters

quilting rulers

self-healing mat

safety pins

seam ripper

fabric sheers

appliqué scissors

flower head pins

You can read more about gluing seams in the Piecing Basics (see page 18), and find resources for purchasing the tips in the Resources section at the back of the book.

Fabric glue sticks are also useful in quilt making, especially in techniques like foundation paper piecing, English paper piecing and machine appliqué, to temporarily keep templates and patches in place.

SCISSORS

Although most of the cutting we do in quilting is with the rotary cutter, it is helpful to have a pair of quality fabric sheers on hand for trimming away excess batting and fabric. Also, small fine-point scissors are extremely helpful for anything from trimming threads to cutting away excess fabric from appliqué blocks. To keep your fabric scissors sharp and in pristine cutting condition, store them separately from your general use scissors and take care to use them only on fabric.

⌐ TIP

I encourage you to invest in high-quality cutting tools that will last a lifetime. Not only will you end up saving money by not having to replace lower grade tools over time, but you'll also benefit from a more peaceful and satisfying quilting experience.

SEAM RIPPER

As much as we may dislike it, "unsewing," ripping out seams, is a reality for even the most seasoned quilters. You can make it less painful by having a high-quality seam ripper on hand. Look for one with a sharp point, an easy-to-hold handle, and a safety cap.

SAFETY PINS

Safety pins are used to baste the layers of a quilt together so they don't shift around when you add the quilting stitches. Fabric stores and quilt shops sell curved safety pins for easier handling during basting, and I usually work with the 1½" (size 2) nickel-plated steel pins.

My homemade pressing table.

IRON AND IRONING BOARD

Although there are irons on the market intended specifically for quilting use, and you may explore these options as you like, you really don't need anything more than a standard steam iron. I've had the same basic Rowenta model for more than a decade and it works wonderfully for patchwork (not so much for pressing wrinkled laundry, though, but that might just be because I hate laundry). To prevent sputtering, staining, or dragging, be sure to clean your iron regularly, inside and out, using the method of your choice.

You may use a standard ironing board to press your patchwork, or, if you like, you can create a tabletop pressing surface by covering a flat piece of wood with a layer of batting followed by washed, color-safe fabric, folded tightly over the edges and stapled. I took this concept a step further in my sewing room, by using an actual tabletop, wrapped in batting and canvas fabric, to create a convenient bar-height pressing table.

STARCH

Spray starch can be used during pressing anytime you want to make your fabrics more crisp and manageable. Starched fabrics are more stiff and behave a bit like paper, which is particularly useful when working with stretchy bias edges or trying to create crisp folds or stiff, easy-to-handle appliqué pieces. I love the Faultless brand, heavy starch.

FUSIBLE WEB

Fusible web is a double-sided, iron-on adhesive used to permanently adhere two pieces of fabric together. We will be using fusible web in three quilts in this book. You can find this product made by a variety of companies at any fabric store, sold by the yard or in pre-cut packages. Look for the paper-backed web, and take care to avoid any products labeled "no sew" because these will gum up your needle.

FREEZER PAPER

Freezer paper is sold by the roll at supermarkets, found near the aluminum foil in the food storage aisle. While it was initially created for wrapping freezer foods, it's also a fabulous quilting tool. One side of the paper is dull and the other feels "waxy" (it's actually plastic coated). You can draw on the paper side, then cut out a shape, and when the paper is ironed onto fabric (shiny side down), it sticks. The temporary adhesion allows the paper to be peeled off and reused several times. We'll be using freezer paper in the Scenic Route quilt on page 62, but I think you'll find even more ways to incorporate it into your sewing and quilting.

My tools of choice.

Selvage edges.

PAINTER'S TAPE

When it comes time to create a quilt sandwich by basting together the layers of your quilt, painter's tape works well for holding the backing fabric piece taut on the floor or on a large table. Why painter's tape? It's strong enough to secure the fabric but will come unstuck with strong pressure, offering a helpful indication that your fabric is being over-stretched. Painter's tape doesn't leave a residue on your fabric or floor, and the bright blue color is easy to spot when it comes time to remove the tape.

Quilting Fabric 101

The fabric most commonly used in quilting and patchwork is called quilting cotton. It is a lightweight 100% cotton fabric that is easy to work with, washable, and comes in a large (dare I say overwhelming) selection of prints and colors. Quilting cotton is sold by the yard off of bolts and has two finished edges at the top and bottom of the fabric called selvages. The selvages are the finished edges of the fabric where the manufacturer often prints information such as the name of the fabric and who the designer was. The distance between the two selvage edges is referred to as the width of fabric (WOF). For most all quilting cottons, the WOF is between 42-45".

When fabric is sold off the bolt, it is cut perpendicular to the selvages, so that 1 yard of fabric measures 36" x 45". When I talk about using yardage, I am referring to fabric that has been cut straight from a bolt and still has both selvages intact, so it has a width of 42-45".

↑ **GOOD TO KNOW** **You will notice that most of my projects use fabric requirements that are based on 42" WOF. Why 42", if the WOF off the bolt is sometimes 45"? I build in a small buffer to account for the selvages that will need to be trimmed, as well as a small margin for error.**

The grain of the fabric refers to the direction of the woven threads. These threads run both parallel and perpendicular to the selvage. When pieces are cut perpendicular to the selvage, they are straight grain. Cuts on the diagonal, are said to be on the bias. Unless noted, it's important to always cut fabric straight of grain; not on the bias, because bias edges are very stretchy and much more likely to become distorted, making piece work difficult and frustrating.

I used an Essex linen/cotton blend for the background fabric in my Potluck quilt to add weight and texture.

Quality Matters

I love bargains just as much as the next gal, but when it comes to fabric, the old saying "you get what you pay for" holds a real element of truth. Quality most definitely varies between generic discount fabrics and designer fabrics, so if there's anything that you skimp on in your quilt making process, don't let it be the fabric. The "hand" of the fabric — the way it feels — is a clear indicator of quality, and is an important thing to consider if you want your quilt to be enjoyed and to last the test of time. High-quality quilting cottons feel soft and substantial in hand, while a lower quality fabric will feel thinner and more crisp, like paper. A higher quality fabric will also be more colorfast with less tendency to bleed or fade, and will even shrink less than lower quality options.

⌐ TIP
Don't be afraid to look beyond quilting cottons when selecting fabric for your quilts. Many natural-fiber woven fabrics work well for patchwork and can add wonderful texture to a design. My favorites include linen and linen-cotton blends, twill, and double gauze. Other options such as poplin, chambray, corduroy, and even denim also work beautifully in a quilt and add loads of character.

Pre-Cuts

Many fabric manufacturers offer convenient pre-cut quilting fabrics in a variety of sizes and shapes, including fat quarters, fat eighths, charm packs (5" and 6" squares), "rolls" of 2½" strips, and 10" square packs. A fat quarter is a quarter yard of fabric that measures 18" x 24", whereas a quarter yard cut straight from a bolt would measure 9" x 45". Fat quarters are among the most popular cuts because they offer a wider (but shorter) section of fabric that can work better for some projects, and also because they are sold in bundles containing every fabric from a particular collection. And let's face it — fat quarter bundles are just plain adorable. If you love a particular line of fabrics, pre-cuts are a quick and easy way to purchase fabrics from that entire line, without having to obtain cuts from twenty or thirty individual bolts. See page 38 of the Color Is Worth a Thousand Words chapter for ideas on incorporating fabric collections into your projects.

Pre-Washing

Pre-washing fabrics remains a very highly debated topic among quilters, and there are a lot of good arguments on both sides of the discussion. It's important to remember that pre-washing is a personal choice, and that someone else may base their decision on reasons that may or may not be valid for you (that includes my preferences as well).

I never pre-wash my fabrics as I find that the crispness of an unwashed fabric (caused by the sizing or starch used in the manufacturing process) makes it easier to work with. Once

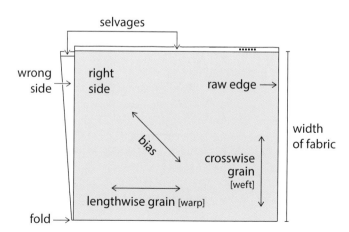

washed, most fabrics become much softer, and I have to counteract this by adding more starch in the piecing process when I press. So, I prefer to just eliminate these extra steps altogether by simply not pre-washing.

Shrinkage is a concern for some, though I have not found it to be a compelling reason to pre-wash. Cotton fabrics do shrink some when washed, but since we aren't stitching garments that need to maintain a precise fit, the small amount of shrinkage that occurs is harmless. Also keep in mind that if you're working with high-quality fabrics, uneven shrinkage among different fabrics is very unlikely.

Even though color bleeding is also very unlikely in high-quality fabrics, if you're working with a very saturated color (like red), it's best to test the fabric for colorfastness before starting your project, just in case. Soak a small piece of the fabric in cool soapy water for thirty minutes, rinse it, then let it dry on a paper towel. If you see any color on the paper towel, pre-wash the fabric and then repeat the colorfast test.

⌕ TIP

For a quick way to prevent possible bleeding, throw a Shout Color Catcher in the wash with your quilt. These little miracles look and feel just like dryer sheets, and will absorb loose dyes in your wash water. Look for them in the laundry section of your local supermarket.

Thread

Selecting thread can be a challenge because there are so many varieties and brands available. I recommend using the highest quality thread that fits within your budget. Many lower quality threads will break easily and get jammed in your sewing machine. You may find that the extra cost is worthwhile to avoid getting frustrated as you sew.

It's helpful to know that the number assigns the weight, or thickness, of a thread. The lower the number, the thicker the thread. I like to work with 100% cotton thread, and typically choose a 50-weight thread for piecing and quilting. My favorite brands are Aurifil, Coats & Clark, and Presencia because they work well with my machine. I recommend testing out a variety of thread brands to see which performs best on your machine.

Pre-cut fabrics are a fun and convenient option.

There is a lot of variety in thread colors, weight, and quality.

PIECING BASICS

Cutting

To cut fabric from yardage, the first step is to square up the fabric to create a straight, neat edge to start from. With the fabric folded in half, wrong sides together and the selvages touching, smooth out any wrinkles; then align your 6½" x 24" ruler perfectly perpendicular to the fold, and trim away the uneven raw edge. **(fig. 1)**

⌐ SAFETY TIP

Always push your rotary cutter (see page 12) away from your body, never toward it. Also, get in the habit of keeping the blade closed unless you are actually making a cut. These blades are unbelievably sharp, and accidentally grabbing or dropping an open blade can quickly put an end to your carefree afternoon of sewing!

What **the scant?**

If you've had your ear to the quilting floor, you may have heard some buzz about "scant" ¼" seams. A scant ¼" seam refers to a seam that is one or two threads shy of ¼". Now, you may ask, as many folks do, why in the world would you ever want to stray from that perfect accuracy? After all, ¼" is ¼", is it not?

Unfortunately, no, and let me explain. If your cutting is accurate, your seam allowances are a perfect ¼", and your pieces are thoroughly pressed open, but you're still finding that your blocks are coming out slightly undersize, then you may need to adjust your seams to a scant ¼". Why? The width of the seam thread itself, and of the fold in your seam allowance, however tiny, does take up space, and in a block, especially a complex one with lots of small patches, this space can add up.

A scant seam accounts for these small amounts of lost width in a seam allowance, and while it shouldn't be a tedious "rule" that stresses you out, if you are experiencing frustration with your patchwork consistently coming out undersize, using a scant seam could be the answer to your woes.

To cut strips, use the markings on the ruler (not on the mat) to cover the width of strip needed, then cut. **(fig. 2)** When cutting, it's always best to position your ruler over the portion of fabric you will be using, instead of over the adjacent fabric. The pressure of the ruler will flatten the fabric and help ensure a more accurate measurement.

To cut strips wider than your ruler, use a square ruler aligned between the raw edge of the fabric and a longer width of yardage ruler to widen the measurement. **(fig. 3)**

To subcut the strips into smaller pieces, rotate the strips 90 degrees on your mat, trim the selvages, then, just as before, use the markings on the ruler to cover the measurement needed and cut. **(fig. 4)**

⌐ TIP

Keep your strips folded in half as you subcut to cut two layers at once. Check out the One-Woman Factory chapter starting on page 36 for more helpful tips on high-efficiency piecing.

¼" Seams

In quilting, seam allowances are always ¼" unless otherwise instructed (and these exceptions are extremely rare). An accurate and consistent ¼" seam is imperative for making sure that your patches and blocks fit together snugly and come out to the correct size. **(fig. 5)**

Stitching a perfect ¼" seam on your machine can take practice. Unfortunately, sometimes presser feet and machine markings can be slightly off, so take the time to measure one of your seams with a clear ruler, just to be sure you're spot on. If your seam is coming up too wide or too narrow, even if by only a few threads, adjust the position of your needle or your fabric until you achieve that perfect ¼" seam.

I suggest marking the correct alignment on your sewing machine's throat plate with a piece of blue painter's tape. Replacing your standard presser foot with a ¼" presser foot, also called a patchwork presser foot, can help alleviate seam allowance struggles, but be sure to test it before fully relying on the foot for precision.

fig. 1 Squaring up.

fig. 2 Cutting strips.

fig. 3 Cutting extra-wide strips.

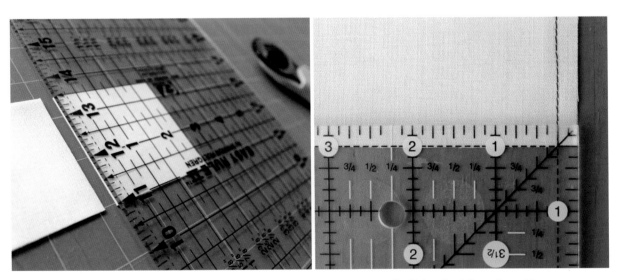

fig. 4 Subcutting a strip.

fig. 5 A perfect ¼" seam is crucial.

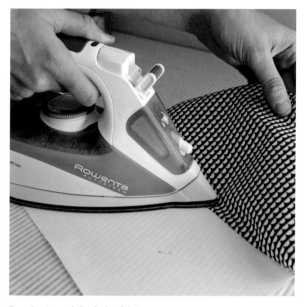

Pressing toward the darker fabric.

Sweet Silhouette wall art project on page 108.

Pressing

Once you've mastered your ¼" seam, it's time to press your piece open. For a nice crisp seam, I set my iron to the hottest cotton setting, with lots of steam. After stitching two pieces of fabric together, but before opening them up, I like to "set the seams" by pressing them from the wrong side, with the pieces still right sides together. This helps the seam to lie more flat once you do open it up and press. Notice that I use the word "press" instead of "iron." In quilting it's important to place the iron directly down onto your fabric, rather than moving it back and forth, which may distort or stretch the fabric.

To press the piece open, lay it on your ironing surface with the seam away from you; whichever fabric you want the seam facing toward is on top. Then lift the top piece and gently press along the seam. Pressing seams toward the darker fabric is a good general rule to go by, since it prevents the seam allowance of darker fabric showing through on the right side. However, if pressing toward the dark would create more bulk, press away from the bulk. In situations where pressing the seam to either side would create an excessive amount of bulk, such as an area where multiple seams meet, press the seam allowance open from the wrong side of the piece.

T **GOOD TO KNOW**
As with any craft, quilting is full of personal preferences, and pressing seams is one of them. Generally, I prefer to press seams to the side, but some quilters choose to press their seams open to reduce bulk. The side-vs.-open seam debate is not likely to end any time soon; I see valid reasoning on both sides. Spend some time experimenting with these options as you piece to determine which method best suits your particular design.

- -

The direction that a seam is pressed can also make an aesthetic difference in the patchwork, other than simply hiding a dark seam allowance. The fabric that the seam is facing toward will subtly stand out from the adjacent fabric because of the added layers of material in the seam allowance. I used this to help add depth and definition to the patchwork in the Sweet Silhouette wall art project.

The best way to achieve crisp, tight seam junctions is to press seams that meet in opposite directions, so that they butt up against each other. This is called "nesting" your seams. By pinning through both layers, right in the sweet spot where the two seam allowances meet, you can create a tight, accurate intersection (yet another reason I prefer pressing my seams to the side instead of open).

Sometimes it takes a bit of forethought to be able to nest seams throughout an entire block or quilt. In most of the quilt projects in this book, the final quilt assembly step calls for pressing odd numbered rows of blocks to the left, and even numbered rows to the right. This is the habit I have developed for assuring that my seams nest between rows for all of my quilts. You may choose to reverse these pressing directions, or come up with your own unique outine for making sure your seams nest.

Pinning and Gluing

To help keep fabric layers from shifting while sewing, I use oodles of flat flower head pins through both layers of fabric. I start by pinning every seam intersection and usually add pins at the ends, and about every 3" in between. Never try to sew over a pin (oh, the sewing machine needles I've broken that way!). Instead, remove each one just before the presser foot reaches it as you stitch.

Can I tell you a little secret? As much of a pinner as I am, my heart has also been captured by glue! When topped with a special thin-tipped nozzle, a bottle of Elmer's washable school glue offers quite a few advantages. To glue-baste your seams, run a thin bead of the glue along the raw edge of one of your pieces, about ⅛" from the edge; then align the top piece, taking care to nest any seam junctions. Then, instantly heat-set the glue by gently running a hot iron over the fabric.

Your pieces will stay put until you are ready to stitch them, and can be easily repositioned. And best of all? No pins to pull out makes stitching a dream, especially on long seams (think joining rows and borders). Whether you're brand-new to quilting or a longtime piecer, I encourage you to give this method a try. I think you'll fall in love with it just like I did!

Nested seams pinned in place.

Glue-basting seams using a specialty tip.

Fabric fused to fusible web, then cut out into desired shapes to use for raw-edge appliqué.

Fuse shapes to the background fabric with an iron.

APPLIQUÉ

Several of the projects in this book are constructed using appliqué, a technique that involves cutting out a piece of fabric into a specific shape, basting or bonding it to the surface of the quilt, and then securing it along the edges with stitching. There are several popular methods for this technique; most of the appliqué quilts in this book use a raw-edge method described here.

Following the manufacturer's instructions, fuse the wrong side of a fabric to the rough side of paper-backed fusible web (see page 14) with an iron. From there, a shape may be traced on the paper side of the web, then cut out with small pointed appliqué scissors or a small rotary cutter. Keep in mind that the image drawn on the paper backing will appear in the final appliqué as a mirror image, so reverse your starting shape if needed (you will not need to reverse any of the shapes for the projects in this book).

Once the shapes are cut, peel off the paper backing to reveal the thin layer of adhesive now bonded to the wrong side of the fabric. Arrange the shapes as desired on your background fabric, then follow the manufacturer's instructions to fuse the shapes in place with an iron. This bond is permanent, so take care that you have your pieces where you want them before pressing.

Check out Scenic Route (see page 62) for detailed instructions on an appliqué technique using freezer paper.

Appliqué pieces may be stitched around their perimeter by hand or by machine. I stitched all of the appliqué projects in this book by machine because I enjoy the modern aesthetic that machine appliqué brings. Machine stitching can be intentionally hidden or minimized, by using monofilament or matching thread and a narrow blind stitch (like I did on Scenic Route), or the stitching can become an intentional

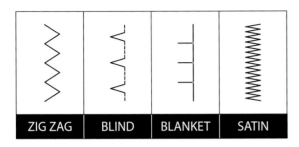

| ZIG ZAG | BLIND | BLANKET | SATIN |

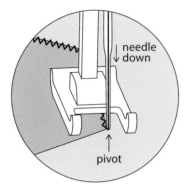

Needle position at a corner.

Scenic Route (see page 62) uses freezer paper.

part of the design, giving the patches more definition with a contrasting color or a more decorative or noticeable stitch.

Regardless of which stitch you choose, keep the bulk of the stitch on the appliqué piece itself, with the right-hand position of the needle just barely hitting the background fabric, just off the edge of the appliqué fabric. When you get to a turn of any kind, stop at the very end of a line with the needle in the down position and to the right, then lift your presser foot, turn the piece, and begin stitching again.

FOUNDATION PAPER PIECING

The Woodland Tree blocks in Scenic Route use foundation paper piecing (see page 62); one of my favorite techniques. This is a piecing method that involves stitching your fabric onto a sheet of paper with a pattern printed on it. The instructions below may seem confusing at first, but stick with me, and you'll see that the results are amazing. This technique is also one of the most forgiving in all of quilting. No precise cutting or accurate seam allowances are required — simply stitch on the lines to create a flawless, intricate block that will look like it took ages to construct.

1. Print or photocopy the template onto standard 20 lb. white paper. Make sure the print settings are set to print at "actual size" — not "scaled" or "shrink to fit". Measure the 1" marking on the pattern with a ruler to double check that the printed pattern is the correct size. Note that the finished stitched block will be a mirror image of the printed template.

2. Cut around the pattern template outside the trim line. The trim line is the very outer line of the template that includes the ¼" seam allowance. If a pattern specifies that you need to add the seam allowance when you trim, then you should cut around the templates outside wherever that seam allowance will be (I've already built in the seam allowance on the Woodland Tree block). You don't need to cut accurately at this point; a rough cut is fine.

3. Perforate the stitch lines on your template using a tracing wheel (most commonly used in garment sewing), or by sewing along them with the unthreaded needle of your machine (I prefer the tracing wheel).

4. Reduce the stitch length on your machine to a 1 or 1.5, which will make ripping off the paper at the end easier. Now for the sewing...

5. Align a piece of fabric directly behind Patch 1, with the printed part of the paper facing you and the right side of the fabric facing away from you. The fabric should extend at least ¼" outside all points of the patch. Hold your paper up to a light source to make sure that the fabric is centered underneath Patch 1 **(fig. 1)**, then secure it to the paper with a dab of fabric glue.

6. Lay the piece on a cutting mat, and fold the paper on the perforated line between Patches 1 and 2. Align a ruler ¼" past the fold line and trim. **(fig. 2)**

7. With the paper still folded, align a second piece of fabric under Patch 2, right sides of the fabric together, so that the top raw edges meet **(fig. 3)**. Patch 2 is folded down toward you at this point and showing through to the wrong side of the paper. Just as before, make sure the fabric extends at least ¼" past the edges of the patch on all sides. Figure 4 shows the back side of the piece in this step.

8. With the printed side of the paper facing you, carefully hold these pieces in place as you unfold the paper, and add a pin. Now, stitch directly on the line between Patches 1 and 2, from beginning to end, removing the pin as you stitch. **(fig. 5)**

9. Flip the paper over so the fabric is facing up, and press the pieces open. **(fig. 6)**

10. Flip back so the paper side is up, and begin this same process again for Patch 3, folding on the line between Patches 3 and 1, then trimming to ¼" **(fig. 7)**. Line up the corresponding fabric piece for Patch 3, open the folded paper, pin, and stitch on the line.

11. Repeat this process until the entire paper template is pieced in numerical order. Press with starch. With the paper side up, trim on the trim line. **(fig. 8)**

12. Carefully remove the paper, one patch at a time. The smaller stitch length will help keep seams intact during this process, but do still take care to support the seam ends with a finger as you tear. **(fig. 9)**

Ϟ **TIP**
Use a seam ripper to remove any stubborn little bits of paper that may remain stuck on the back of your piece.

- -

If you would like more visual instruction on this technique, check out my video demonstration in the October lesson of the 2012 Craftsy Block of the Month series. www.stitcherydickorydock.com/craftsy-bom/

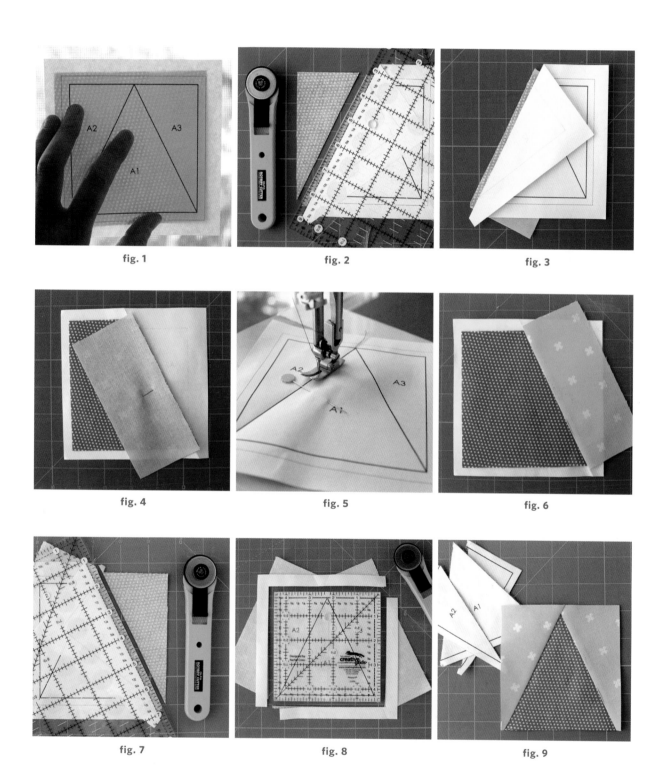

fig. 1

fig. 2

fig. 3

fig. 4

fig. 5

fig. 6

fig. 7

fig. 8

fig. 9

SASHING AND BORDERS

Sashing refers to the fabric between blocks and a border is fabric that frames the perimeter of the quilt. Several of the quilts in this book include sashing and borders. Both are great ways to make a quilt larger and to add definition and interest to the design. There are so many possibilities for getting creative with these, like adding cornerstones between the sashing, or adding multiple borders.

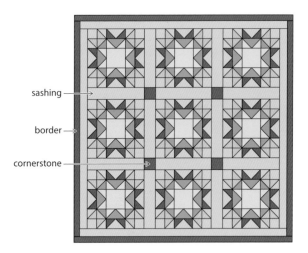

sashing

border

cornerstone

Cutting and Joining Strips

If the length of the edge where the strip will be added is more than 42", you need to stitch multiple strips along the short edge. Use either a straight seam or a 45-degree seam (see page 32), depending on the print you are working with and which you feel will create a less noticeable seam in the quilt. Trim the selvages and stitch the strips together, creating one long strip. If you're adding vertical sashing, cut the strips to the height of your unfinished blocks.

⌐ GOOD TO KNOW
Quilting patterns often refer to "finished" or "unfinished" blocks. The block's unfinished measurements are before being pieced, so it includes a ¼" seam allowance on all sides. The finished dimensions refer to the size of a block after those perimeter seam allowances have been subtracted. So if you are constructing a block that the pattern states is 12" finished, you will end up with a block that is 12½" unfinished and 12" after you've stitched it into a quilt.

Measuring

Measuring long strips of fabric or the edge of a quilt top with a measuring tape can be a futile business. Fabric lies differently than a tape measure, making it difficult to get accurate measurements. For this reason, I have not included lengthwise border or sashing measurements for any of the quilts in this book. Instead, I prefer an organic approach in which the fabric strips themselves are the measuring tape. Let me explain...

Lay out your pressed quilt top (or, for sashing, your center row of sashed blocks) and gently smooth it out. Then lay the strip across the center of your quilt in the direction that it will be going. Pin one end of the strip to the edge of the quilt. Smooth the strip along the quilt until it's nice and flat, but not stretched. Use fabric scissors to cut the strip at the edge of the quilt, taking care to make a straight 90-degree cut. You can cut all the strips that will be going in the same direction using this measurement. For borders, measure and cut the side strips first; then after you've stitched them to the quilt top and pressed them open, measure and cut the top and bottom strips.

To ensure an accurate measurement, take care that your border strip is positioned perfectly straight across your quilt. An easy way to do this is to find the center points on both sides of your quilt by folding the quilt in half and marking the centers with a pin or fabric marker, then running your border strip from one center point to the other. Align sashing strips in the same way, making sure they are straight across your center row of blocks.

Pinning and Stitching

Now that you have strips cut to the correct length, it's just a matter of pinning them on to your quilt without any shifting or stretching. To do this, fold your strip in half and mark the center point with a pin, then do the same for the quilt. Match up these two points with a pin, then pin at each end. Work your way across the strip, adding pins every 2" to 3".

Stitch the borders to the quilt with ¼" seam as usual, removing pins as you go, and press open so the seam is facing toward the border piece. As stated previously, sew on the side border strips first, then measure, cut and sew on the top and bottom border strips.

FINISHING YOUR QUILT

After all the time and effort you put into piecing a fabulous quilt top, don't let it gather dust on a shelf. Finish it right away so that it can be put to use and enjoyed! In this section I'll show you how to turn your pieced top into a ready-to-snuggle quilt by basting and quilting it to the batting and backing, then finishing the raw edges with a tidy binding.

Batting

A quilt is like a sandwich. It has three layers: the pieced quilt top, the batting, and the backing. Even though we usually spend an enormous amount of time focusing on the top of the quilt, what's inside it is equally important because it has a significant impact on the quilt's final look, feel and longevity. Take the time to familiarize yourself with batting choices, and make your selection thoughtfully so that you end up with a quilt that looks and feels just as you envisioned it would.

Batting is available in a variety of materials, including cotton, wool, bamboo, silk, polyester, and cotton/polyester blends. I strongly suggest working with natural materials over synthetic ones, and I particularly love cotton, wool, and bamboo/cotton blends for my quilts.

COTTON

Cotton is the most popular quilt batting choice for many reasons. It launders well, and does shrink up a little bit, giving quilts that distinct "crinkly" look. That, and the fact that cotton is a thinner batting, makes it an excellent choice if you're going for a lovely flat, vintage look. Cotton is wonderful for machine quilting, and it is also the most breathable of batting materials and yet insulating and warm.

WOOL

Wool batting creates the warmest quilt and offers a thicker loft than cotton, but it is still flatter than synthetic options. It resists creases, drapes beautifully, and works well for both machine and hand quilting. Wool can require special washing instructions, however, so be sure to read the manufacturer's instructions before you make a decision.

BAMBOO

Bamboo and bamboo blends are relatively new to the market. They are quickly becoming popular because, like cotton, bamboo is breathable and wash-friendly. It is easy to machine quilt and is also naturally antibacterial. Bamboo is more expensive than cotton, but is still a great choice for an heirloom quilt.

POLYESTER

Polyester does not shrink or flatten, so quilts will always remain "puffy" and really hold their shape. It isn't as breathable as natural batting options but it is very economical.

COTTON/POLY BLENDS

Blends are typically 80% cotton and 20% polyester. They aren't as thin as 100% cotton batting, but are a less "puffy" alternative to 100% polyester batting, with many of the great characteristics of cotton.

Different batts (that word just makes me giggle) also require different densities of quilting in order to keep their shape and remain intact inside your quilt over time. Read the manufacturer's recommendations to be sure you are choosing the right batting for your project.

I used leftover blocks to piece a unique backing for this quilt.

Another unique improvised backing using up tiny scraps.

Backing

Quilt backings can be made from a single cut of extra-wide fabric or even an elaborately pieced work of art nearly rivaling the front. The choice is up to you. Use up extra blocks, piece together leftover yardage, create an entirely new design, or just choose a single fabric that you love.

For the quilts in this book, I listed yardage requirements for a single cut of fabric, with one vertical seam down the center. Feel free to forgo my backing yardage requirements in favor of your own pieced backing if you are so inclined. Keep in mind that for quilting, your backing needs to be 4"–5" larger than the quilt top, on all four sides.

To construct backing from a single piece of yardage for a quilt that is between 40" and 72" wide, start with a piece of fabric that is twice the length of your quilt, plus 18". For quilts that are wider than 72", triple the length of your quilt, plus 27". The chart (opposite) is a handy resource when you want to make a single fabric backing.

Piecing a single fabric backing is quick and easy. First, open up the yardage and trim off both selvages. I love to rip the selvages off! Make a 2" snip at the selvage edge. Grip the selvage in one hand and the fabric with the other, then rip with all your might until the entire selvage is removed. This method does create some fraying, but it can be minimized by pressing and lightly starching the ripped edge.

With selvages now removed, fold the yardage in half to find the center point along one of the previously selvaged edges, then cut the piece in half, either by the "snip 'n' rip" method described above or with a rotary cutter. Stitch the two pieces along the long edge, right sides together, with a ½" seam allowance and press the seam open.

⌐ GOOD TO KNOW

Most woven fabrics can be ripped straight of grain in both directions. Not only is ripping a great way to blow off steam and bewilder any onlookers, but it's also a sure way to create a perfectly straight and on-grain cut, every time.

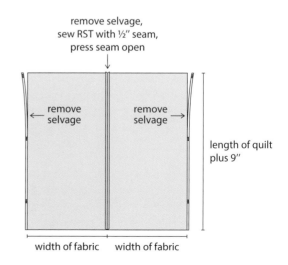

remove selvage,
sew RST with ½" seam,
press seam open

← remove selvage   remove selvage →

length of quilt plus 9"

width of fabric   width of fabric

Making a Quilt Sandwich

This is the portion of the quilt-making process where the three layers of a quilt come together in large, dramatic fashion. You'll need a sizable hard, flat surface, large enough to spread your quilt out on and still be able to move around the perimeter. For me, this means my front sitting room, and it always involves finding a temporary new home for some furniture. Make sure whatever place you choose is an area that you can keep free of muddy paws and curious little fingers, and ideally offers some great light.

⌐ GOOD TO KNOW

The basting process outlined below is for quilting your quilt on your regular home sewing machine (hip hip hooray for that!) or by hand. Longarm quilting, however, requires the layers of a quilt to be loaded individually onto the large frame of the machine, so this basting step isn't necessary. See page 32 for more information on the longarm quilting option.

1. Spread the pressed quilt backing onto the floor with the right side facing down. Tape the perimeter of the quilt to the floor using painter's tape about every 6". Start on one side, then move to the opposite side, pulling the backing taut but not stretched. Repeat with the remaining two sides until the backing is completely smooth and secured.

2. Spread a layer of the batting over the backing, smoothing out any wrinkles. There is no need to tape the batting layer because the texture of the fibers will keep it in place.

3. Finally, lay the quilt top on the batting, right side up and centered, then smooth out any wrinkles.

4. Starting at the center of the quilt and working your way out, insert curved safety pins through all three layers, about every 6". I like to place my pins in an organized graph pattern consisting of evenly spaced rows and columns. This way, I'm sure not to miss any spots and my spacing is consistent, which makes removing the pins during the quilting process more predictable. It can also prove helpful to put some thought into your quilting design before pinning. Sometimes you can intentionally place pins in areas where you may not be stitching as much, or at least outside of a direct stitching path.

5. Once you've pinned your entire quilt, remove the tape, and you're ready to start quilting on your home machine!

LENGTH OF QUILT — YARDAGE REQUIRED

30	2 ¼	47	3 ¼	64	4 ¼	81	5
31	2 ¼	48	3 ¼	65	4 ¼	82	5 ¼
32	2 ½	49	3 ¼	66	4 ¼	83	5 ¼
33	2 ½	50	3 ½	67	4 ¼	84	5 ¼
34	2 ½	51	3 ½	68	4 ½	85	5 ¼
35	2 ½	52	3 ½	69	4 ½	86	5 ½
36	2 ½	53	3 ½	70	4 ½	87	5 ½
37	2 ¾	54	3 ½	71	4 ½	88	5 ½
38	2 ¾	55	3 ¾	72	4 ½	89	5 ½
39	2 ¾	56	3 ¾	73	4 ¾	90	5 ½
40	2 ¾	57	3 ¾	74	4 ¾	91	5 ¾
41	3	58	3 ¾	75	4 ¾	92	5 ¾
42	3	59	4	76	4 ¾	93	5 ¾
43	3	60	4	77	5	94	5 ¾
44	3	61	4	78	5	95	6
45	3	62	4	79	5	96	6
46	3 ¼	63	4	80	5		

My favorite way to remove the selvage is to rip them off.

Pin basting in a grid keeps me organized.

the hive lives on

One hundred fifty years ago out on the prairie, when a quilt was ready to be quilted, a community came together for an all-day "quilting bee" extravaganza. Friends and neighbors brought their entire families. They ate, they danced, and, my, did they quilt. They quilted till their fingers were numb, on their own quilts and on their neighbors'. Why? To socialize, yes, but also because quilts are large! That's a whole lot of space to fill with artful, visible stitches (especially by hand), and many hands helped to lighten the load.

Today, we have our trusty electric machines by our sides, making quilting so much quicker and easier; yet, even with a machine, it can still feel like a big undertaking. So when it comes down to you and your quilt, sitting at your dining room table in front of your little machine, trembling, and asking yourself what in the world you've gotten yourself into, I want you to remember that historic "quilting bee" community. It still exists, a quilting community ready and willing to be your hive. They may not arrive at your doorstep in a covered wagon, but they will undoubtedly lend support, encouragement, and loads of tips and instruction, if you will only seek them out.

Get to know your local quilt shops and sign up for any machine quilting classes offered. Take online classes, dive into the mountain of helpful books available on the topic, attend workshops and conventions. Read blogs, start a blog, join Instagram, and allow the ever-growing, thoroughly passionate modern-day "quilting bee" — both online and in your local area — to be a source of learning, of ideas, of inspiration and most of all, of friendship.

My Viking extension table designed to fit my machine.

Quilt as Desired

It's not surprising that these three simple words, "quilt as desired," can manage to strike fear into the heart of even the most enthusiastic of quilters. We are so eager to buy our fabrics, to cut them into a million pieces, and then stitch them up again, but when it comes to quilting our quilts, the fact is, it's very easy to feel overwhelmed. Well, I'm here to tell you that not only can it be done on your home machine, but it's a whole lot of fun! Quilting physically holds the layers of a quilt together and adds surface texture, but it can also be as expressive and inspired as the piecing itself. The basics I offer here will help you get started on the right foot, but keep in mind that this just scratches the surface of an enormous topic.

Work Space

The first key to machine quilting at home is setting up an effective work space. In addition to good lighting and a comfortable chair, the surface area around your machine is also important. Adequate space behind and to the left side of your machine will allow room for your quilt to be spread out while you are stitching, so an L-shaped table or desk setup is ideal (keep in mind that desks and tables can be temporarily pushed together to create a work surface when you need it, and then be moved back when you're done).

Photo and sewing table by Marta Strzeszewski.

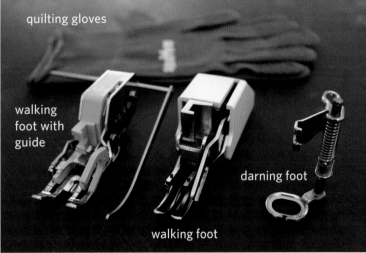

quilting gloves

walking foot with guide

darning foot

walking foot

Sewing machine essentials for quilting.

It's also helpful to have your sewing table pushed up to a wall, so that your quilt can't fall off the back of it. Maintaining control of the quilt is essential, which means avoiding a setup that may cause your quilt to hang off the edge of the table, interrupting the ease of the stitching.

The larger the flat, level surface around the bed of your machine, the better. Extension tables are a widely available option and the Internet is also full of great tutorials on fabricating your own flat sewing surface.

Machine Quilting Tools and Supplies

A walking foot is a large, boxy presser foot that allows your project to be fed through the machine from both the top and bottom, minimizing the shifting of your quilt's layers while you quilt. This foot is used in stitching straight (or very gradually curved) lines, and most come with a guide piece that enables you to follow any existing seam or line in the quilt as you stitch.

A darning foot is a small, round foot that uses a spring-like action to smoothly glide over the surface of a quilt. This foot is used during free-motion quilting, a technique that involves lowering or disengaging your machine's feed dogs and instead using your hands to freely move the quilt in any direction.

Rubber-tipped quilting or craft gloves can offer a better grip on your fabric, and products like the Supreme Slider, among others, can help reduce friction between the machine bed and your quilt.

⌐ GOOD TO KNOW Keeping a bowl or jar next to your machine gives you a handy place to toss your safety pins as you remove them.

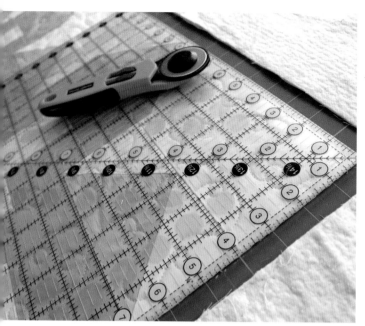

Squaring up the quilt sandwich.

Straight-Line Quilting

I adore the modern, clean look of straight-line quilting. There are so many ways to customize and adapt it to fit your particular tastes and project. One technique that I particularly enjoy is "echo quilting," stitching just outside the seams. I like this technique because it requires no marking and it does a great job of playing up the geometry that already exists in a quilt. Or, if you choose, you can use echo quilting to create a whole new shape in the quilt.

⌐ RESIST THE DITCH

Stitching in the seams of a quilt is called "stitching in the ditch." Although it's a very well-known technique, I encourage you to stay away from it whenever possible. Stitching in the ditch hides those precious quilting stitches that you work so hard to create, and it tends to make a design look more "puffy" and dated by indenting the perimeter of a patch or block, but without creating any surface texture. If you're looking for a simple straight-line design that's similar to stitch-in-the-ditch, try echo quilting instead, and highlight seams in your quilt by stitching just outside them rather than in them.

Free-Motion Quilting

This is where the fun really begins! Once you cover or lower your feed dogs and pop on a darning foot, all of a sudden you and only you are the one making the quilt move beneath the needle, and there is nothing stopping you from going in any direction. Even though the feed dogs are disengaged, you are still in control of the speed using your foot pedal. It can take some time to get used to this freedom and you will need to practice matching the speed of your foot with the movement of your fabric, in order to create even stitches. Practice is the only thing between you and quilting any design you can possibly fathom.

⌐ SMOOSH 'N' ROLL

Methods for physically wrangling your quilt during the machine quilting process vary. I prefer to casually (and fairly aggressively) smoosh my quilt into the throat of my machine as I'm working. Some quilters prefer to roll their quilts as they work in rows. Experiment with what feels comfortable to you. Whichever you choose, if you start in the center of your quilt and work your way out in any direction, you'll never have more than half your quilt in the throat space at any one time.

Longarm Quilting

If you have a major deadline, or you just aren't enchanted by the idea of quilting at home, sending your quilt top to a longarm quilter might be the best option for you. A longarm is an industrial quilting machine. The quilt layers are loaded onto rollers and stretched taut (like a scroll), while the longarm machine glides on a track between the rollers, stitching the layers together. Many quilt shops host professional longarm quilting services, and the Internet is also packed with professional quilters who offer mail-out services. Some quilt shops also provide longarm training and allow you to quilt on their machine for a fee.

Squaring Up

Once your quilt is quilted, it's time to prepare it for binding by "squaring up." To square up your quilt, lay one corner of it on your cutting mat, then use your largest square ruler and a rotary cutter to create a nice sharp 90-degree corner, leaving no excess batting beyond the quilt top fabric. Continue around the perimeter using a long straight ruler for the sides and the square ruler for the corners. If any edges of the quilt top have stretched or distorted during the quilting process, they will be trimmed straight in this step. You can also use your ruler to measure the size of the blocks around the exterior of the quilt, making sure that your trimming leaves them at a consistent size.

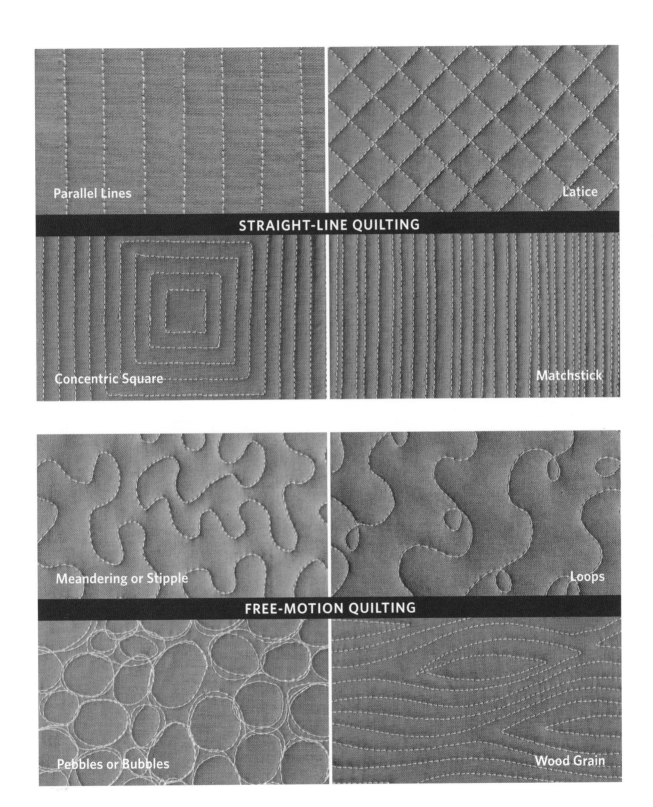

Parallel Lines

Latice

STRAIGHT-LINE QUILTING

Concentric Square

Matchstick

Meandering or Stipple

Loops

FREE-MOTION QUILTING

Pebbles or Bubbles

Wood Grain

Binding

There's nothing like a tidy binding to finish off a special quilt. I'm just crazy about binding! Here's my favorite method, which uses both machine and hand stitching:

1. Calculate the perimeter of your quilt, then add 20". Divide this number by 42, and if you get a decimal (you almost always will), round up to the nearest whole number. This is the number of 2½" x WOF strips you'll need to cut from your binding fabric. (I've given you the number of strips to cut in each of the projects in this book, but it's always handy to know how to calculate it yourself).

2. Stitch all the strips end to end on a 90-degree angle, then trim off the excess with scissors. The 90-degree seam minimizes bulk, so that the seam doesn't stand out on the finished binding. There is no need to trim off the selvage edges before joining the strips, because they will be trimmed off with the excess.

3. With wrong sides together, press the entire strip in half lengthwise, pressing the seams open as you go.

4. Starting in the center of one of the sides of your quilt top, with your sewing machine, stitch the binding to the edge of the quilt using a ⅜" seam, leaving a 10" tail at the beginning.

5. When you reach a corner, stop ⅜" from the end. Pull the quilt out from under the needle without clipping the threads, rotate it clockwise, preparing to stitch the next side. Fold the binding up and away from you while holding the fold with your finger, and then fold it back down again, in line with the edge of your quilt.

6. Continue stitching on the binding around the entire quilt. When you reach the first side again, stop about 12" before the place where you started.

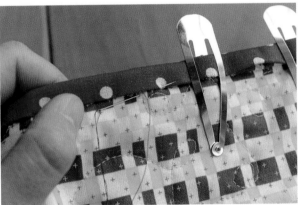

7. Lay both binding tails flat along the edge of the quilt so that they meet at the center of the 12" space. The tails should be right sides together, pointing away from the surface of the quilt. Pin the tails together at the exact point where they meet, taking a very small pin bite through only the inner layers of the binding. I refer to this point as the "critical point".

8. With the critical point still pinned, open up both ends of the binding and place them right sides together and at a 90-degree angle, scrunching up the quilt to create slack in the binding.

9. Stitch a diagonal line across the path where the edges of the bindings cross. Pull the quilt flat so that the binding re-folds and make sure that it lies flat against the quilt, then trim to a ¼" seam allowance and press the seam open.

10. Lay the quilt flat and stitch the remainder of the binding on, securing the seam at both the beginning and end.

11. Lastly, wrap the binding over to the back side of the quilt and hand stitch down with a blind stitch, folding and securing miters at the corners.

ONE-WOMAN FACTORY

My mother grew up in a small Midwestern town, amid vast corn fields and modest brick homes. Her mother, my grandmother, led the 4-H club in which Mom picked up the love of sewing that was destined to be passed down our family tree. When she was 21 years old and home from college for the summer, she worked as a seamstress for the local hospital. Down in the hospital basement, beneath a flickering glow of fluorescent lights, she mended linens and sewed little newborn gowns for all the bouncing new babies. It has always fascinated me to hear about her assembly-line process. There she was, all by herself, lovingly stitching these little gowns, truly keepsakes in their own right, not one by one, but 50 at a time.

My mother.

In my own way, I feel like a one-woman factory too. I stitch quilts instead of dresses, blocks instead of hems; but just like my mom, I have a lot to get done in a limited amount of time. Just because quilting is a heart-filled art form doesn't mean it needs to be tedious or inefficient. By streamlining the piecing process and using some factory-style tips and techniques, you can get more done in less time and feel a whole lot more relaxed along the way. Below are a few of my favorite tips.

High-Volume Tips

Most steps in the piecing process can be done en masse. It's helpful to determine which steps might be good candidates for high-volume methods before you start your project.

GROUPING TASKS TOGETHER

Chain piecing may be the most popular time-saving technique and for good reason. Stitch your patches, one after another, without cutting threads in between. When stitching parallel seams, like 2-at-once half-square triangles or 4-at-once flying geese, the chain piecing can pay off twice. Don't clip the threads after your first round of seams. When stitching the second round, the patches will practically feed themselves into the machine. After stitching all the units, clip the threads to separate them.

Cutting, marking and pressing can also be done in large groups. With a sharp blade and solid pressure, up to four layers of fabric can be cut at once without compromising the accuracy of the cuts. If you have a long ruler, such as 6½" x 24" (often used for cutting yardage), you may line up not only multiple layers but multiple rows to be cut at once.

For patches that require drawing marked lines, use the lines on your cutting mat to line up and mark multiple patches at once.

Chain piecing.

High-volume cutting.

High-volume marking.

Organization

If you're making a quilt with many blocks and different fabrics, it might be tempting to forgo a high-volume process and opt for a one-block-at-a-time approach. Time constraints may force you to step away from a project for a few days, even weeks, and you don't want to get mixed up when you return. Resist the urge to skip the factory-style system; in the end, the saved time will pay off. By simply employing some organizational-friendly techniques, you can use the high-volume piecing methods and save oodles of time — even if you anticipate gaps in your piecing schedule.

SWATCH CARDS

Using a swatch card to keep larger projects organized is one of my absolute favorite time-saving tips. Glue a small piece of fabric to a card to indicate which fabrics are being used in which blocks. Not only will it help you remember which fabrics you selected for which blocks — it will actually give you the freedom to be able to incorporate high-volume piecing methods without fear of creating a disastrous jumbled monster of mixed-up patches. With your trusty swatch card by your side, you can cut, stitch, pin, and press hundreds of patches at once, all for different blocks, and you'll always know what goes where.

SORTING

Once the high-volume steps are out of the way and it's time to start constructing blocks, sorting patches can be another helpful way to keep things organized as you move forward with your project. Paper plates are especially handy for keeping patches sorted and ready to go whenever you are.

Baggies, baking tins, baskets, and trays are also great ways to keep blocks and patches organized. Experiment to find out what works best for you and your project.

MARKING

Nothing is more frustrating than taking the time to painstakingly tweak your final quilt layout, only to have your blocks get mixed up. (Ask me how I know this!) After one too many mix-ups, I now take photographs of all of my layouts before I begin piecing and I also mark my blocks using water-soluble markers or stickers. If you use the marker method, test your marker first on a scrap to make sure that it truly will wash out, and that it isn't the kind that disappears after a period of time. Some markers work better on certain fabrics than others. If you can, try a few different brands for each fabric you are piecing with until you are happy with the results. If you use the sticker method, consider reinforcing them with a pin to ensure all your great organization won't slip off.

My swatch card for the Potluck quilt.

Paper plates keep patches sorted and handy.

Stickers will keep blocks and rows in order.

A COLOR IS WORTH A THOUSAND WORDS

Ideas for Inspired Fabric Selection

Let's talk about fabric selection, shall we? Truth be told, this is my favorite part of the quilting process. Quilt making feels just like coloring did when I was kid. A quilt-to-be is a crisp blank sheet of paper just begging for color, and a luscious rainbow of fabrics are my crayons — bright, happy, and full of possibility. With so much to choose from, narrowing the fabric field can be intimidating, but it can also be empowering, and even therapeutic.

The colors and fabrics you choose bring your projects to life. They can reveal your mood or create a new mood. They can make a statement and if you let them, they can tell a story, your story. In this section I offer tips and ideas for thoughtfully selecting fabrics you love, in dynamic combinations, that will speak to your heart today and inspire you for years to come.

A Key to Dynamic Patchwork

There is a wide world of color theory out there and we could get scientific about fabric selection if we wanted to. I could tell you about chromaticity, luminosity, tints, tones, and shades, but honestly, I'd rather just cut to the chase. The key to dynamic patchwork boils down to one simple thing: contrast. For our purposes, contrast is the juxtaposition of colors and prints. What happens when we create contrast? It intensifies the properties of each element and creates a more dynamic design.

What does "dynamic" actually mean? Think powerful, compelling, influential, lively, electric. If your patchwork is meaningful, if you're going to pour your heart into it and you want it to speak, to tell your story, and to show who you are, "dynamic" is just the ticket.

A mix of color families, contrasting values, prints and solids, and small and large scale fabrics, all work well to create a balanced quilt design.

PRINTS VS. SOLIDS

A favorite print can be the perfect inspiration for creating the color palette for an entire quilt. Simply by finding the colors used in the inspiration fabric (the selvege dots are an excellent tool for color-matching) and using a selection of supporting fabrics in those colors, all but ensures that your quilt design will be successful. It can be difficult to focus on purchasing solids when there are so many irresistable prints available from so many talented designers. Still, I recommend creating a robust stash of solids in a few of the colors you use most frequently in your piecing. Not only will incorporating solids make your prints stand out, but they also give the eye a much-needed rest in a busy design. Incorporate solids to draw even more attention to your favorite prints and to add a sense of

"calm" to a potentially hectic-feeling quilt. Solid fabrics are usually much cheaper than prints too!

The Make Your Move quilt (see page 76) pairs some beloved prints with coordinating solids.

LIGHT VS. DARK

The "value" of a color refers to how light or dark it appears. Using a mixture of light-, medium-, and dark-valued fabrics will create wonderful contrast and make areas of your quilt "pop." Similarly valued fabrics, on the other hand, will blend together, de-emphasizing the individual patches or shapes.

LARGE SCALE VS. SMALL SCALE

Mixing small prints with medium and larger prints will allow each of the prints to shine in its own way. A design that uses similarly scaled prints can end up looking and feeling more chaotic as the fabrics tend to compete with one another.

Keep in mind that the size of your project and/or your patches may also determine the scale of prints that works best. For example, in the Family Secrets recipe binder (see page 126), my patches are only 1" across, so I stuck to smaller prints and used other methods to create contrast.

⌐ TIP

Photography comes in handy when evaluating contrast. Turning a color image to black and white instantly reveals which fabrics appear darker and which are lighter.

Black and white photography sheds light on the color value.

COOL VS. WARM

Colors from green and blue families are considered "cool" hues, while those leaning toward red and yellow are "warm" hues. Mixing cool colors with warm colors adds wonderful contrast and character.

FLORAL VS. GEOMETRIC

Along with value, hue, and scale, the type of print can affect contrast. Mixing geometrics, such as stripes and dots, with other styles of prints, such as florals, will add definition to your design, giving your prints more impact.

Scrappy quilts are casual and friendly.

Scrappy Go Lucky

Scrappy patchwork uses little pieces of fabric left over from other projects. If adding more and more fabrics to your pile seems to make it prettier and prettier, then you might be a scrappy addict, just like me. Perhaps this tendency goes back to my love of vintage quilts, which were predominantly scrappy because of the need to use and re-use every bit of fabric available. No online shopping or fabric stores bursting with bolts 'n' bundles in the 1920s and 1930s!

There's something comforting to me about this look. It feels casual, friendly, and unassuming. There are no "rules" with scrappy — in fact, the less "planned" the better — so you're free to use whichever and however many prints you like. Most of the projects in this book have a scrappy look, because that is the aesthetic that feels most comfortable and pleasing to me. Follow your own tastes and embrace or forgo this style choice in your own quilts.

You may also notice that some of the quilts in this book are designed around color or value groupings, like Sunday in the Park (see page 88), Popped (see page 48), or Home Is Where the Heart Is (see page 122). These projects call for a variety of prints from a single color family (reds, yellows) or from a single value (light, medium, or dark fabrics). These types of quilts have a way of making larger areas of color stand out, add order, focus and definition to the design, yet still maintain a scrappy look.

For example, in the Sunday in the Park quilt, the focus of the overall design is on four defined colors creating a simple lattice or plaid-type pattern, yet I was still able to incorporate almost fifty different prints, giving the quilt that scrappy feel I so love.

Store Fabrics by Color

I've found that the way I organize and store my fabrics has a significant impact on how and what fabrics I choose for my projects. My instinct when I first began accumulating quilting fabrics was to keep collections together (in truth, I could hardly bear to take the pretty ribbons off and unstack such lovely bundles!). But at some point in time, I made the leap to separating my precious collections and now I store everything by color and in color order. Admittedly, it felt a little like ripping off a Band-aid, but once it was off, I was so glad I'd done it. I instantly noticed a boost in my creative juices, and in a way, it transformed how I see color in general. All of a sudden I was pairing together fabrics that I never before would have noticed and creating some fabulous combinations. I felt more control, more freedom, more inspiration.

So consider sorting and storing your fabric by color. Also, if at all possible, try to store your fabrics within view of your work space, or at least within view of one another, as it can be difficult to recall by memory exactly which juicy plums or poppy corals you might have at the ready, and it's

Organize scraps by color to save time and hassle.

Possible color grouping for a scrappy quilt.

handy not to have to dig through boxes or bins to find out. I realize that not everyone has a designated sewing space, let alone a cabinet to store their fabrics in, but I encourage you to take the essence of this idea and shape it to fit your particular storage reality.

⌐ TIP
Webster may define "scrappy" as literally made up of scraps, but that doesn't mean your quilt needs to be. Feel free to create your scrappy look out of whatever you have: yardage, pre-cut fabrics, vintage fabrics, or even vintage sheets. Or… just use scraps.

My stash is organized by color.

Inspiration Is All Around

We really don't have to look far to find inspiration in the world around us — and it's certainly not limited to the aisles of your favorite fabric shop. Look to your surroundings for color inspiration and you're likely to start viewing the world through a whole new set of eyes. Remember: anything is game. From the wildflowers on the side of the road to a book, a garment, or a vase — nearly anything can inspire the colors you choose for your quilt.

⌐ GOOD TO KNOW

Your camera can be your best friend when it comes to capturing inspiration for fabric selections. Keep a running file of these shots on your phone or computer so that you have a personal source of inspiration to turn to whenever the need arises. You can also snap photos while pairing up fabrics, to help you remember great combos. Seeing the fabrics in a photo may change your perception of how they would look together.

Fabric Collections: A Very Good Place to Start

This may seem totally counterintuitive, after I've just advised you to sort your fabrics by color, but I've found that one great way to get the ball rolling, especially if you're feeling a pull toward a particular fabric collection, is to go with that instinct and use the fabric collection as a starting point. There's no need to reinvent the wheel — if you like it, you like it. I adore fabric collections, but I also want to encourage you not to limit yourself to working within single lines of fabric. Just because a group of fabrics has a cute name and is tied up in pretty bow, doesn't mean they're inseparable, or that you're somehow defiling them by adding your own personal stamp. Maybe try removing a few prints, or even one color altogether, then start adding to the mix — perhaps introducing a new color or colors, or building on colors that are already present. Before long, you may find that you've stumbled onto a totally unique selection that would not have come together without having had that tangible starting point.

Trust Yourself

Having worked in several quilt shops over the years, I can't tell you how many times I've seen quilters just throw their hands up in frustration and say, "But how do I know if these fabrics look good together?" My response? "Trust yourself." Yes, you can memorize color theory concepts and carry a color wheel around with you, and that knowledge certainly could prove helpful and fuel creativity, but at the end of the day I know what I like, and I think you do too. Trust that. Incorporate color theory if you choose, but don't let "rules" get in the way of an organic fabric selection process. Countless gorgeous, beloved quilts have been conceived with absolutely no regard for color theory, and you know what? That's 100% okay.

Inspiration: True Colors fabric line by Heather Bailey for FreeSpirit Fabrics.

Resulting personalized selection.

The best thing about memories is making them.

MEMORY MAKERS

The projects in this section are all about packing up, snuggling in, spreading out, and spending some serious quality time with the ones you love. A quilt can cover a bed, but it can also spark a new tradition or trigger some fun times. It could stay folded up in the closet, but imagine it tucked around your legs, toted to the park, or spread out in the back of an old truck, soaking up more and more meaning with each precious memory. My intention behind each of these projects is to encourage as many of those moments as possible, in my family and I hope in yours. I hope you love making them as I did, and I hope you love looking at them, but most of all, I hope you love using and enjoying them every day — and that in some special way these little patches of fabric sewn together, will play a part in the telling of your story.

"The happiest moments of my life have been the few which I have passed at home in the bosom of my family." —Thomas Jefferson

POPPED

Pieced by Amy Gibson and Karen O'Connor, quilted by Susan Santistevan

Jammies on, lights dimmed, popcorn popped, and a special quilt to warm four sets of squirmy toes, all lined up on the couch — that's our weekly family movie night, and it's one of our favorite traditions. We love how casual and easy this event can be: nothing fancy, just a chance to decompress together as a family after an especially rough or busy day. There are no shortages of squeals breaking out when one of us declares "family movie night tonight!" And if we had a late lunch, even better. Maybe we'll just skip dinner altogether and splurge on a big fat bowl of homemade popcorn and some rocky road ice cream. It's the best.

We watch new movies, old movies, movies we've watched 1,001 times and never get sick of. And oh, how I love pulling out the old classics that I enjoyed as a child. Hearing them giggle at Don Knotts, or hum along with Shirley Jones, watching them stare in disbelief that old mom and dad actually know all the lines to "Singin' in the Rain" (aka "super cool new movie") — not only is it just ridiculously fun, but it brings us together. And I love together.

Finished Quilt Size: 60½" x 72"

Finished Block Size: 12" x 12"

Materials

Yardage requirements are based on 42" wide fabric

4 yards background fabric

Scraps or (3-5) ¼ yard pieces, from each of 6 distinct color groups (number each color group from 1 to 6)

1¼" paper hexagon templates

NOTE: You will need 360 templates for this quilt. I recommend puchasing pre-cut hexagon papers in bulk (see page 136), or copy and cut out your own templates using the grid on page 53.

4¼ yards backing fabric

½ yard binding fabric

67" x 78" batting

Washable fabric glue stick

Matching thread

Hand sewing needle

Cutting

From background fabric, cut:

(10) 12½" x WOF strips

    subcut into (30) 12½" squares

From each of 6 color groupings, cut:

(60) 3¼" squares, for a total of 360 squares

From binding fabric, cut:

(7) 2½" x WOF strips

I **GOOD TO KNOW**

For nice even numbers, use 12 prints per color and cut 5 squares from each, or use 15 prints per color and cut 4 squares from each. You may cut a different quantity of squares from each individual print, as long as your total per color is 60.

> **This quilt is composed of 30 blocks. There are 10 blocks each of 3 different color placements.**

Constructing a Hexagon

1. Dab a small amount of washable fabric glue stick in the center of the wrong side of a 3¼" square of fabric. Center the template on the wrong side of the square.

2. Fold a corner of the square over the side of the paper hexagon. While holding the corner in place with your finger, fold an adjacent edge of the fabric square over the paper hexagon.

3. With the paper side of the hexagon facing you, push a needle, threaded and knotted with a contrasting colored thread, up through the paper template and through all layers of fabric at the folded corner.

4. Fold an adjacent corner in the same fashion, hold it in place, then take another stitch through the fabric layers and paper template at that fold.

5. Work your way around the hexagon, taking large basting stitches at all 6 corners. When you reach the 6th corner, take a small extra stitch, going back and forth through the layers once. Cut the thread leaving a 1" tail and without knotting.

I **GOOD TO KNOW**

If you're having trouble getting smooth edges and sharp points on your hexagons, try starching your squares first (see page 14).

Piecing the Popcorn Kernel Units

6. With the paper still inside, place 2 hexagons from the same color group right sides together. Pull a needle threaded with a matching knotted thread between the fabric and the paper on the wrong side of one of the units, coming out at the tip of one of the corners (hiding the knot on the wrong side of the fabric).

7. Whipstitch the 2 pieces together along an edge, taking care not to go through the paper. Try to catch only a few threads from each hexagon with each stitch. When you reach the end of the edge, tie a quilter's knot by pulling the needle through a loop of thread 3 times and then pulling it tight.

8. Add a third hexagon to the unit, whipstitching one of the sides adjacent to the seam, but instead of knotting at the end of the edge, continue on to the remaining side by gently bending the joining hexagon in half.

9. Stitch all 120 kernel units: 20 from each of the 6 color groups.

10. Press and starch the right side of each unit, then pull out the basting stitches and carefully remove the papers, taking care to maintain the folds.

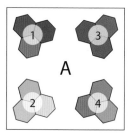
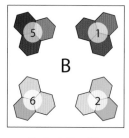
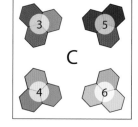

Blocks A, B and C.

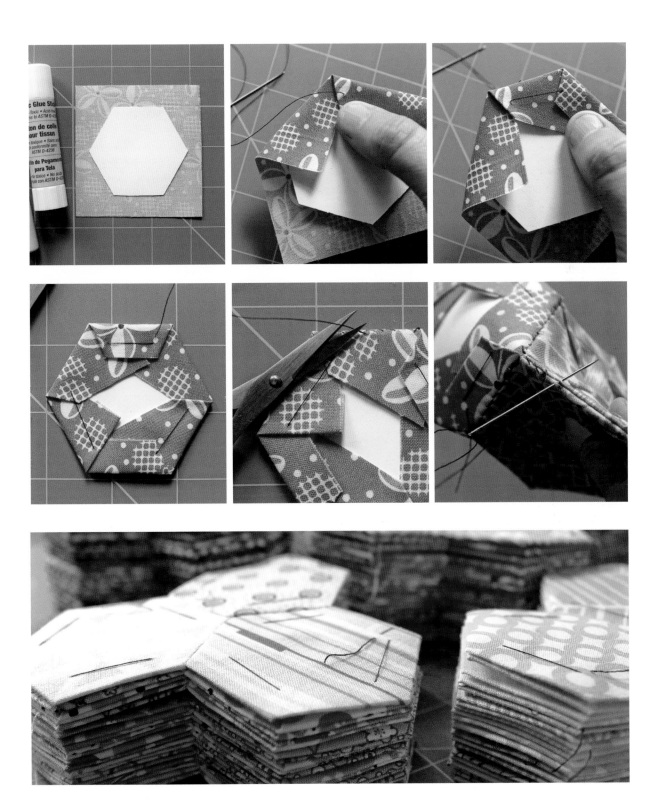

Appliquéing the Hexagon Units

11. Glue-baste (see page 21) or pin 4 hexagon kernel units to each background square, aligning each unit 1" from the corners and using a ruler to check that the placement is straight.

⌐ GOOD TO KNOW

Use two rulers, one on top of the other, rather than just one, to check both alignments at once. This way, half the kernel will still be exposed (instead of fully covered by a ruler), making it much easier to adjust the alignment.

- - - - - - - - - - - - - - - - - - - -

12. Appliqué the unit to the background squares using your favorite appliqué method. I chose to appliqué my hexagons using a machine zigzag stitch in a matching colored thread.

⌐ GOOD TO KNOW

Save time by appliquéing all similarly colored hexagon units at once, switching thread colors only when you've stitched all the units of a particular color on each of the blocks and are ready to move on to the next thread color.

- - - - - - - - - - - - - - - - - - - -

Assembling the Quilt

13. Stitch the blocks together into 6 rows of 5 blocks each alternating the directions you press the seams, then stitch rows together. Take care to pin at each seam intersection and press all seams to alternating sides.

Finishing

14. Using the methods described in A Patchwork Primer beginning on page 27, piece the backing, make the quilt sandwich, baste, quilt as desired, and bind.

meaning
in the making

Details help make your family movie night extra special. Set up a concession stand, then, let young children take your "order" and deliver your snacks. Movie theater-style popcorn bags are inexpensive and available at most party stores. Schedule an official intermission, to give everyone a chance to stretch, use the facilities, and talk about the movie.

POPPED
1¼" Paper Hexagon Templates
Photocopy at 100%

POTLUCK

Pieced by Amy Gibson, quilted by Linda Barrett

When I look back on my favorite family gatherings, on the traditions I grew up with and that continue to be the source of many of our most enjoyable times together, there is one very strong thread flowing through them all: food. From marshmallows toasting over a crackling backyard campfire to my mother's Christmas morning egg casserole, our family comes together over food, again and again. Yes, we need to eat, we need nourishment; but more than that, we need to connect. We need to tell old stories and laugh at ourselves. We need to make new memories. We need opportunities to share with and listen to those loved ones who perhaps don't live in our home and who we don't see every day — even those loved ones who only live across town, yet we run the risk of "losing" to the distance of busy schedules.

When I was younger, I gobbled up those chocolaty s'mores and just assumed that these times just happen by themselves. But the truth is, getting together requires intentional focus. So in our family, we are always keeping our eyes open for opportunities to gather the troops and feed them. It doesn't take much more than that. Any and every birthday, young or old, we gather. The start of summer? We gather. A Tuesday night and someone has a homemade pie in the oven? We gather. We gather and we bring food, and everyone always has something to share — fresh tomatoes and basil from the garden, a green bean casserole or a bottle of wine.

Webster defines "potluck" as "food or a meal that happens to be available without special preparation or purchase" and also as "a meal, especially for a large group, to which participants bring various foods to be shared". And that's just what this quilt is all about: seizing times whenever we can, for any reason at all, to gather, to share, and to eat.

Finished Quilt Size: 58" x 58"

Finished Block Size: 15" x 15"

Materials

Yardage requirements are based on 42"-wide fabric

2 yards background fabric

¼ yard each of 36 varied prints

NOTE: You will use 4 prints for each of the 9 blocks. Be sure the fabrics you select for each block contrast with one another. Select fabrics from four separate color groups (nine prints per color) so your blocks will really stand out. See Figure 1 for print placement.

You may use the same print twice without the need for additional yardage.

½ yard for cornerstones and second border

3⅔ yards backing fabric

½ yard binding fabric

64" x 64" batting

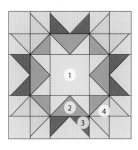

fig. 1

Cutting

From background fabric, cut:

(3) 3" x WOF strips

  subcut into (36) 3" squares

(3) 3⅜" x WOF strips

  subcut into (36) 3⅜" squares

(2) 6¼" x WOF strips

  subcut into (9) 6¼" squares

(6) 3½" x WOF strips

  subcut into (12) 3½" x 15½" rectangles

(5) 2½" x WOF strips

Trim selvages, stitch end to end, and set aside.

From each of the nine Print 1 fabrics, cut:

(1) 5½" square

(4) 3⅜" squares

From each of the nine Print 2 fabrics, cut:

(1) 6¼" square

(2) 3⅜" squares

From each of the nine Print 3 fabrics, cut:

(4) 3⅜" squares

From each of the nine Print 4 fabrics, cut:

(6) 3⅜" squares

From cornerstone and second border fabric, cut:

(1) 3½" x WOF strip

  subcut into (4) 3½" squares

(6) 2" x WOF strips

From binding fabric, cut:

(6) 2½" x WOF strips

✐ GOOD TO KNOW A swatch card (see page 37) would sure come in handy right about now. Once you've decided which prints you want in which position for each of your blocks, making a swatch card will enable you to cut and piece all your units in one large group without worrying about fabrics getting mixed up. Delightful!

Constructing the Blocks

The Flying Geese

There are 8 flying geese units in each block, constructed in groups of 4 geese. Each group of 4 geese requires (1) 6¼" square and (4) 3⅜" squares.

1. On the wrong side of each of the four small Print 1 squares, draw a diagonal line. Align 2 of these squares on the large Print 2 square, right sides together, so the drawn lines stretch diagonally across the large block. Stitch ¼" on both sides of this drawn line **(fig. 2)**. Cut the unit in half on the drawn line and press the patches open. In the same way, align the 2 remaining small squares on each of the 2 pressed units, right sides together, so that the drawn line is perpendicular to the seam **(fig. 3)**. Stitch ¼" on both sides of the line. Cut in half on the drawn line, creating 4 flying geese units **(fig. 4)**. Press open. Each unit should measure 3" x 5½".

2. Create 4 additional flying geese units from the 6¼" background square and the (4) 3⅜" Print 3 squares.

The Half-Square Triangles

There are 12 half-square triangle (HST) units in each block, constructed in pairs. Each pair of HSTs requires (1) 3⅜" square from each of the two prints in the unit.

3. Pair each Print 2 with a Print 4 square, and the remaining (4) Print 4 squares with background squares, and follow the HST contstruction method illustrated on page 79 of Make Your Move to create the 12 HST units for each block. Each unit should measure 3" square.

4. Referencing Figure 5, stitch the star block together, pressing seams open or away from the bulk. Repeat to create 9 blocks. Square blocks to 15½".

Assembling the Quilt

5. Referencing Figure 6, assemble the quilt top, adding the sashing pieces between the blocks, then joining the rows with sashing and cornerstone strips in between. Take care to match and pin at seam intersections. Press seams toward sashing.

6. Next, add the borders using the long background and border fabric strips, stitching the sides of the inner border first, then the top and bottom of the inner border, and then moving on to the second border in the same fashion.

Finishing

7. Using the methods described in A Patchwork Primer beginning on page 27, piece the backing, make the quilt sandwich, baste, quilt as desired, and bind.

meaning
in the making

Spice up your potluck by adding an unexpected theme to help get your guests thinking outside the box about their dishes. Some of my favorite ideas are: an international potluck, breakfast for dinner, finger foods, seasonal foods, and soul food. Not only will the food selection be refreshingly unique, but it's also a great way to break the ice.

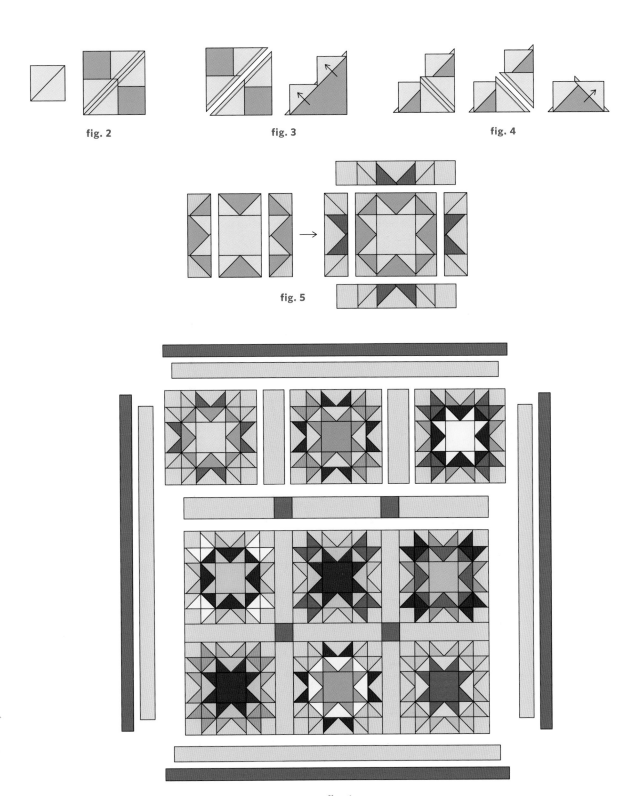

fig. 2

fig. 3

fig. 4

fig. 5

fig. 6

STARGAZER

Pieced by Amy Gibson, quilted by Susan Santistevan

Admittedly, I am always in fifth gear. I work hard and I play hard, but even when it's play, it's almost always somewhat productive. We're eating out as a family, but we're also filling our bellies without having to scrape macaroni off the floor after dinner. We're walking to the park, but we're also getting exercise. We're playing cards, but we're also learning sportsmanship and practicing math or memory skills. See what I mean? Fun, yes, but productive. So the inspiration behind this design comes from a very true place of challenge for me: quality time by way of doing absolutely nothing.

That's right, nothing. The only goal is being together, focusing on one another, sharing, dreaming, laughing, with absolutely nothing else on the agenda. No TV or media, no "activity" to speak of — just being together, resting, and connecting. I call this concept "stargazing." It's like lying on our backs, shoulder to shoulder, counting stars or watching clouds, and just being together without distraction. In a light-speed world with 211 billion things to do 24/7, it can be tough to unplug from the pace, but I think it's a precious necessity, worthy of our time. I hope this quilt will inspire you, as it does me, to remember to stargaze once in a while with the ones you love. Buy a hammock, blow some dandelions, spread out a quilt in the bed of a truck and relax... just be.

Finished Quilt Size: 66" x 72"

Finished Block Size: 6" x 6"

MATERIALS

Yardage requirements are based on 42"-wide fabric

4¼ yards background fabric

¼ yard each of 13 light-colored prints, or 13 precut 2½ wide strips (for the small stars)

⅓ yard or a fat quarter for each of 7 light-colored prints (for the large stars); may be the same or different prints as the small stars

4¼ yards backing fabric

⅝ yard binding fabric

72" x 78" batting

Cutting

From each of the 13 small star prints, cut:

(1) 2½" x WOF strip
  subcut each into (15) 2½" squares

From each of the 7 large star prints, cut:

(1) 6½" x WOF strip
  subcut each into (5) 6½" squares

From background fabric, cut:

(15) 6½" x WOF strips
  subcut into (85) 6½" squares
(20) 2½" x WOF strips
  subcut into (312) 2½" squares

From binding fabric, cut:

(8) 2½" x WOF strips

Constructing the Blocks

1. Take (3) 2½" print squares from each of the 13 small star prints and set aside. Take 1 square from each of the (7) 6½" large star print squares and set them aside. These will be the centers of your stars.

2. To create the large star points, place a 6½" print square on top of a 6½" background square, right sides together, so that one edge of the print square is crossing over a corner of the background **(fig. 1)**. Make sure that at least ¼" of print fabric extends beyond the background square on

either side of that corner. The precise angle of this placement should intentionally vary from block to block, giving the stars their "wonky" look.

3. Stitch a ¼" seam where the print fabric crosses the background fabric, then press the print square open. **(fig. 2)**

4. Turn the block over and trim the print fabric to match the corner of the background fabric. Repeat to create 4 large star point blocks in each of the 7 large star print fabrics.

5. Repeat Steps 2–4 on the adjacent corner of the background square using the remainder of the same print square. **(fig. 3)**

6. Repeat for the remaining 27 large print squares (excluding the 7 centers previously set aside). Set aside. **(fig. 4)**

⌇ TIP

The degree to which your star points overlap one another where they attach to the center of the star is a personal choice that you may want to play around with. When the points do overlap, it produces a more traditional star shape, while points that don't touch can create a more abrupt, edgy look. I had fun experimenting with the angles, so my quilt contains some of a variety of overlap.

7. Repeat Steps 2–5 to create the small star points, using the remaining 2½" print squares (excluding the 45 small star centers previously set aside). You will have 12 small star point blocks for each of the 13 prints.

8. Referencing Figure 5, assemble the small star blocks using a 9-patch layout. Press seams away from the pieced patches. Repeat to create a total of 39 small stars.

meaning in the making

If you're new to this wonky, irregular style of piecing, it may feel a bit uncomfortable. Sometimes "letting go" of ultimate control of your patchwork can turn out to be therapeutic, and unexpectedly open doors to creativity you didn't know you had. Embrace the liberating imperfection of improvisational piecing, and, most importantly, have fun!

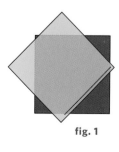

fig. 1

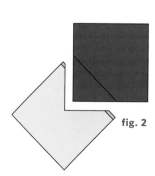

fig. 2

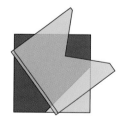

fig. 3

fig. 4

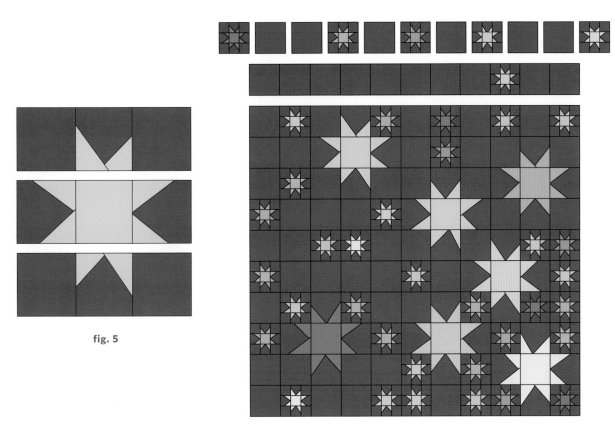

fig. 5

fig. 6

Assembling the Quilt

9. On a floor or design wall, lay out all your blocks referencing Figure 6, including 39 small stars, 7 large star centers, 28 large star point blocks, and 58 plain background squares. Stitch 12 rows of 11 blocks each. Press seams of odd-numbered rows to the left and even-numbered rows to the right. Pin rows together at each seam intersection, then stitch rows together and press seams to the side.

Finishing

10. Using the methods described in A Patchwork Primer beginning on page 27, piece the backing, make the quilt sandwich, pin-baste, quilt as desired, and bind.

"It is good to have an end to journey toward;
but it is the journey that matters, in the end." — Ernest Hemingway

SCENIC ROUTE

pieced by Amy Gibson, quilted by Linda Barrett

The year our twin boys were born, my husband and I took a trip to visit family on the East Coast. We had planned to take our family of six for a cross-country visit over Christmas. As we started making arrangements, it didn't take long to realize that we wouldn't be hopping on an airplane this time and jetting across the country. A mountain of baby and toddler gear, undesirable seating arrangements, and costly airline tickets meant we'd be taking the "scenic route" — driving the 1,500 miles in our trusty van. Road trip with four kids under the age of five? It sounded like a recipe for disaster...self-inflicted torture even.

But we did it, and you know what? As much as we cherish our special times with extended family, and the glorious holiday that it was, what really made that trip unforgettable was the journey. We sang. We listened to audio books. We played games. We sipped milkshakes for breakfast in Missouri and had waffles for dinner in Kentucky. We laughed and talked about anything and everything, and by the time it was all over, it was almost as if our drive had been the destination all along. And that's what this quilt is all about: the wonderfully winding scenic route. The path may be longer, but it can also be paved with priceless memories, and I wouldn't trade those memories for the world. Here's to packing up, settling in for the drive, and remembering that the journey matters.

Finished Quilt Size: 52" x 52"

Finished Block Size: 6½" x 6½"

MATERIALS

Yardage requirements are based on 42"-wide fabric

1⅛ yard gray fabric
(for the road)

¼ yard each of 28 prints

3½ yards backing fabric

½ yard binding fabric

58" x 58" batting

Roll of freezer paper

White 20 lb. paper
(or whatever printable paper you prefer for foundation paper piecing), a total of 8 sheets

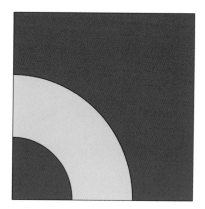

Road block.

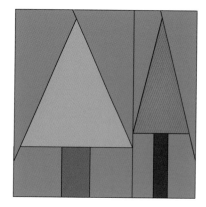

Woodland tree block.

Cutting

From gray fabric, cut:
(7) 5" x WOF strips

From each of the 28 prints, cut:
(2) 7" squares

From background fabric, cut:
(2) 2" x 5" rectangles
(2) 3" x 1½" rectangles
    Set aside for the small tree background
(2) 3" x 5½" rectangles
(2) 2½" squares
    Set aside for the large tree background

From the print fabric, cut the following units for each of the 8 tree blocks:
    For the large tree top, cut:
    (1) 5½" square
    For the large tree trunk, cut:
    (1) 2" x 2½" rectangle
    For the small tree top, cut:
    (1) 3" x 5" rectangle
    For the small tree trunk, cut:
    (1) 3" x 1¼" rectangle
    From binding fabric, cut:
    (6) 2½" x WOF strips

> This quilt is composed of two different blocks: curvy road blocks and woodland tree blocks. There are 56 road blocks, and 8 tree blocks.

Constructing the Blocks

Road Blocks

1. Transfer the Road Template (see page 69) onto a piece of thin cardboard or template plastic and carefully cut out the shape.

2. Trace around the cardboard template onto the dull (paper) side of the freezer paper and cut the shape with a small rotary cutter or scissors. Repeat until you have 56 units.

3. Using a hot iron, press the shiny (waxy) side of the freezer paper units to the wrong sides of the 7 gray strips, aligning the straight edges of the paper with one of the raw edges of the strip and leaving a 2¼" space between the papers along this straight edge **(fig. 1)**. These templates are reusable and may be peeled off and repositioned as needed.

4. Using a small rotary cutter, cut out the template shapes, adding ¼" for seam allowance along both curved edges, but cutting on the drawn line for the straight ends. **(fig. 2)**

5. Peel off the paper template from the fabric and flip the paper over, so that the wrong side of the fabric and

the dull side of the paper are touching. Align the paper in the exact same way it was before. **(fig. 3)**

6. Using the tip of a hot dry iron and your fingers, carefully fold the seam allowances over the curved edges and press them in place. Repeat to create a total of 56 road units. Take care not to run the iron over the exposed paper, only on the seam allowance. **(fig. 4)**

7. Position a road unit onto each 7" print square, right sides up, with raw edges aligned. Press to "fuse" the curve to the square (the freezer paper between the layers of fabric provides a temporary light adhesion). To ensure a secure fusion, after pressing on top, flip over the block and press from the back as well. Repeat for all 56 blocks.

8. Stitch the road units to the squares along the curved edges using a machine appliqué stitch (see page 22). In this case, it is especially necessary to use as narrow a stitch as possible, so as to catch only a small amount of the paper in the seam. On my Viking Sapphire, a blind stitch 1.5mm wide and 4.5mm long worked perfectly. Test and adjust your stitches on a scrap first. **(fig. 5)**

9. Flip the blocks over and use your finger to separate the print fabric from the paper. Cut away the fabric between the seams, leaving ¼" allowances. Gripping the seams to stabilize them, remove the papers. **(fig. 6)**

10. Discard the papers **(fig. 7)**

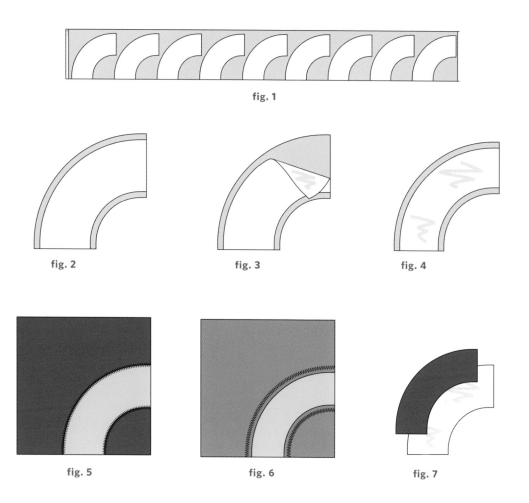

fig. 1

fig. 2

fig. 3

fig. 4

fig. 5

fig. 6

fig. 7

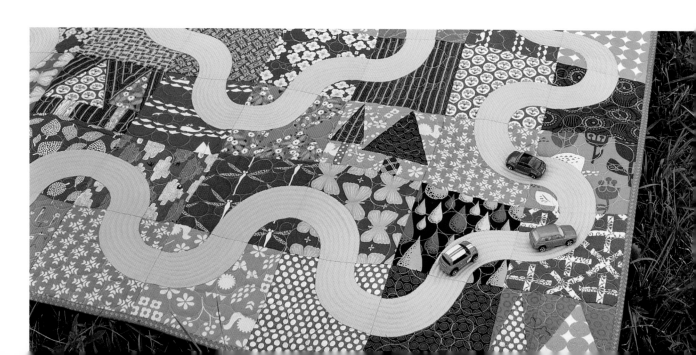

meaning
in the making

Quilting, like life, is a journey from point A to point B. A stack of fabrics turns into a quilt. But how? The process is just as important as the end result, and sometimes I take the scenic, or less traveled, route because I enjoy the ride. I chose this curved piecing method to construct this quilt because the process is so relaxing for me. Same result, different route. I so enjoy the stress-free pin-less stitching, and the opportunity to do the trimming by hand, as I cozy up to watch a good movie.

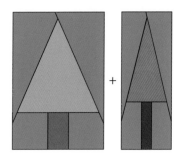

fig. 8

fig. 9

⌐ GOOD TO KNOW

Not only can you save the paper templates to reuse on down the road (pun intended), but you can also save the excess curved pieces trimmed from the back of the blocks. How pretty would these be as appliqués in a design of their own? Make another quilt top, or incorporate them into the backing of your Scenic Route quilt!

Woodland Tree Blocks

11. Make 8 photocopies of each of the 2 Woodland Tree Templates (see pages 68 and 69). Cut the templates on the cut line. Piece the individual tree units following the foundation paper piecing guidelines (see page 24).

12. Once the tree units have been stitched and trimmed to the cut line, carefully remove the paper and stitch each Unit A to its coordinating Unit B. Stitch 4 of the blocks so that the large tree is on the left **(fig. 8)** and 4 of the blocks so that the large tree is on the right. **(fig. 9)**

⌐ TIP

See page 36 of the One-Woman Factory section for tips on keeping your blocks organized as you stitch them together.

Assembling the Quilt

13. On a floor or a design wall and referencing Figure 10, lay out all of the blocks using a flat quilt image as a guide. Stitch 8 rows of 8 blocks each. Press seams of odd-numbered rows to the left and even-numbered rows to the right. Pin rows together at each seam intersection, then stitch rows together and press seams to the side.

Finishing

14. Using the methods described in A Patchwork Primer beginning on page 27, piece the backing, make the quilt sandwich, pin-baste, quilt as desired and bind.

fig. 10

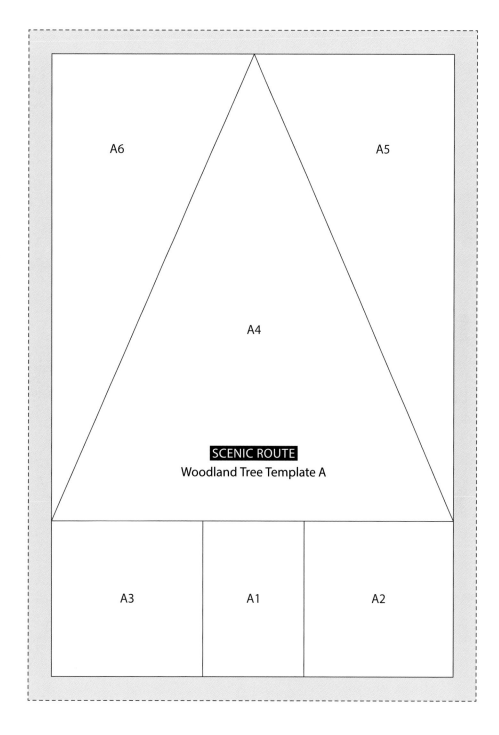

A6   A5

A4

SCENIC ROUTE
Woodland Tree Template A

A3   A1   A2

Photocopy at 100%

– – – cut line

——— stitch line

■ seam allowance

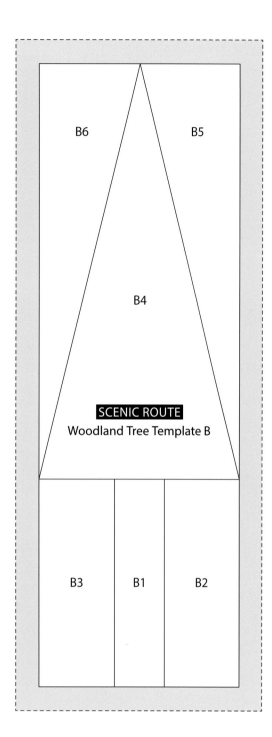

B6   B5

B4

SCENIC ROUTE
Woodland Tree Template B

B3   B1   B2

Photocopy at 100%
- - - cut line
—— stitch line
seam allowance

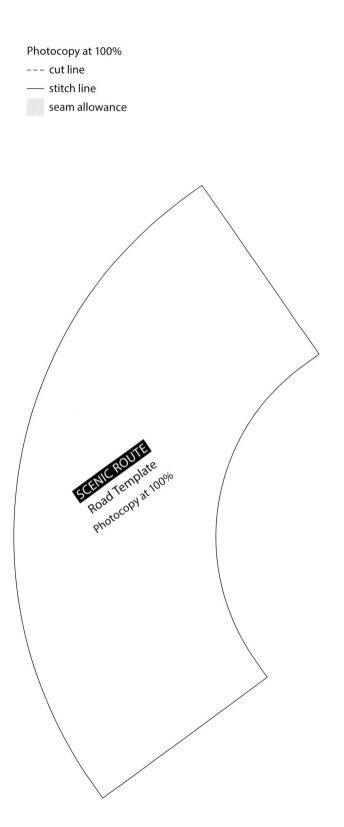

SCENIC ROUTE
Road Template
Photocopy at 100%

"You can never get a cup of tea large enough or a book
long enough to suit me." — C.S. Lewis

ONCE UPON A TIME

Pieced and quilted by Amy Gibson

The experts tell us we should read to our children for at least twenty minutes every day. They tell us it helps build their vocabulary and foster their ability and desire to read. And it does. But what they don't tell us is how utterly mutual the enrichment really is. Instead of being an obligatory task that we do for our kids' health and wellness, like reminding them to finish their carrots or helping them brush their teeth, it's a gathering, a ritual we all look forward to and are involved in.

Our reading is often scattered throughout the day, but it's the pre-bedtime book soiree that has become the main attraction. What started with shorter picture books grew to chapter books and series. Each evening, as my husband would plop himself down in the armchair and open up the next endearing chapter of Ramona the Pest or Mrs. Piggle Wiggle, I found myself coming up with reasons to be in the room — folding laundry, changing sheets, or just working on a little hand stitching. Reading aloud was a light and we were the moths: it drew us in. And when the parent who isn't even doing the reading is there too, an amazing thing happens. All of a sudden we're showing our kids the magic of reading — not just by reading to them but by enjoying it with them, as a family.

This whimsical pocket body pillow was born out of a desire to pay homage to family reading time, and, admittedly, also out of a desire to reduce the number of books I have to fish out from behind the beds! And I must say, we score on both accounts.

Finished Size: 52" x 18" (fits most standard-size body pillows)

Materials

Yardage requirements are based on 42"-wide fabric.

Pocket fabrics from scraps (or charm squares/mini charm squares), enough to end up with:

(13) 4½" squares or larger

(52) 2½" squares or larger

3 yards exterior fabric

1½ yards lining fabric

⅓ yard binding and ties fabric

51" x 56" batting

Standard-size body pillow, approximately 50" x 20"

Cutting

From scraps, cut:
(13) 4½" squares
(52) 2½" squares
From binding fabric, cut:
(3) 2½" x WOF strips
(1) 2" x WOF strip

Construction

1. Stitch the 2½" patches into 13 blocks of 4 patches each, then construct a 2-block x 13-block panel, alternating a 4-patch with a solid patch **(fig. 1)**. Match and pin seam at intersections.

2. Remove selvages from lining fabric, then trim to 52½" x 39".

3. Stitch the patchwork panel to the lining piece along the 52½" side. If your patchwork fabrics are directional, stitch the bottom of the patchwork piece to the lining. This will be the front of your quilt sandwich. **(fig. 2)**

4. Create a backing for the quilt sandwich using the exterior fabric, placing the seam as indicated. **(fig. 3)**

5. Using the methods described in A Patchwork Primer beginning on page 27, make the quilt sandwich, pin-baste, and quilt as desired. Trim the quilt to the size of the front piece. Machine stitch the binding to the front side and hand stitch on the back. Leave the ends raw. Set the excess binding aside for now.

6. With the exterior side facing up, fold the patchwork pocket up so that the fold at the bottom of the pocket exposes ½" of the lining side of the quilt **(fig. 5)**. Mark a center line from binding to fold with a water-soluble pen. In the same way, mark the center line of both halves of the pocket. Pin

and stitch on these lines, securing the seam at the binding and reinforcing with extra stitching at pocket opening.

7. Take the 2" x WOF strip for the ties, trim the selvages, cut it into 4 equal lengths. Following the steps on page 93 of the quilt carrying strap instructions from Sunday in the Park, make 4 topstitched ties, each with one end finished and the other end raw.

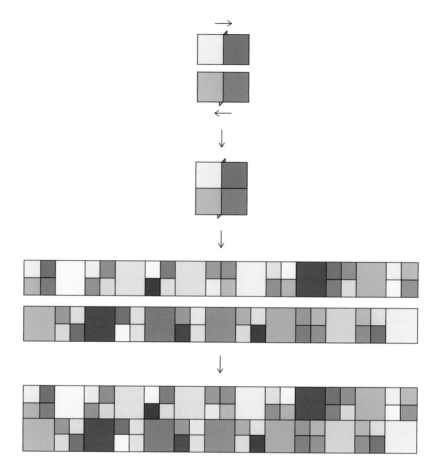

fig. 1

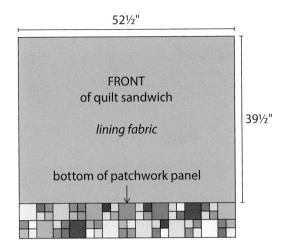

52½"

FRONT
of quilt sandwich

lining fabric

bottom of patchwork panel

39½"

fig. 2

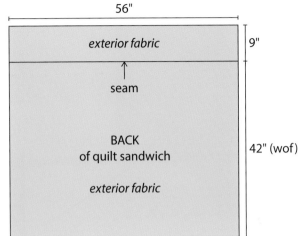

56"

exterior fabric

seam

BACK
of quilt sandwich

exterior fabric

9"

42" (wof)

fig. 3

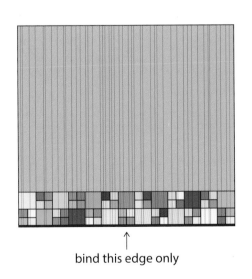

bind this edge only

fig. 4

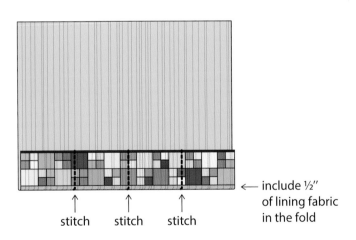

← include ½"
of lining fabric
in the fold

stitch   stitch   stitch

fig. 5

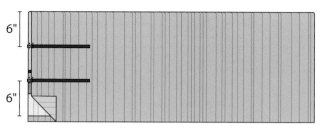

fig. 6

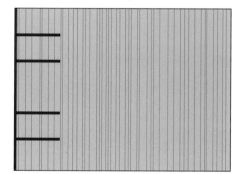

fig. 7

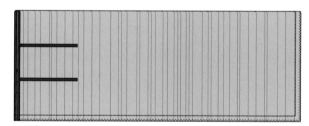

fig. 8

8. Fold the piece in half lengthwise so that the lining side is facing out. On the left end of the piece (or whichever end you wish the opening to be), measure 6" from both the top and bottom, excluding a ½" at the bottom of the pocket where the lining fabric is folded up. Pin the raw edge of a tie even with the raw edge of the pillow at these two points on the lining side of both layers. Baste using a ⅛" seam. **(fig. 6)**

9. Open up the pillow cover and attach the remaining binding to the exterior side of the end with the pinned ties. Reinforce the ties with a bit of extra stitching as you stitch the binding on. **(fig. 7)**

10. Finally, fold the pillow cover in half again, right sides together and matching the top with the bottom edge, then pin along the two remaining raw sides. Stitch a ½" seam, securing at the beginning and end. Serge or zigzag stitch the seam allowance to prevent fraying.

11. Turn the cover right side out and press if needed. Insert the pillow and tie the opening closed with a bow.

meaning **in the making**

Offer an even stronger feeling of ownership over this special pillow by letting your family lay out the squares for the pocket. You can facilitate by pre-selecting a large quantity and variety of squares, (more than you will need for the project), and then letting your family choose exactly which ones to use and where they will go. This way, you keep some control of the fabrics, while still giving your family a say in the process, and the pride of having "designed" it themselves.

MAKE YOUR MOVE

Pieced by Amy Gibson, quilted by Susan Santistevan

Something extraordinary happens, at least it does in our house, when we get the whole family together, turn off the TV and phones, order a pizza, and pull out some favorite games. It's game night, and it's all about quality time. Whether we're just doing puzzles or getting serious over some brainy board games, somehow this ritual helps us to stop zoning out and start tuning in to each other. We're not socializing online or doing housework. We're all in, focused, and making moments together. Teaching moments. Rolling on the floor laughing moments. Priceless moments.

This quilt is all about carving out time to laugh and talk and play with an intentional presence and focus, free of electronics. Other than a good old-fashioned meal around the table, few activities seem to kindle these times like an evening of games. So roll the dice, spin the wheel, choose a card, or spread out this quilt for an active, large-scale game of beanbag checkers. But whatever you do, have fun!

Finished Quilt Size: 72" x 72"

Finished Block Size: 9" x 9"

Materials

Yardage requirements are based on 42"-wide fabric.

1¼ yards white fabric

1¼ yards gray fabric

⅛ yard each of 24 prints

4½ yards backing fabric

⅝ yard binding fabric

78" x 78" batting

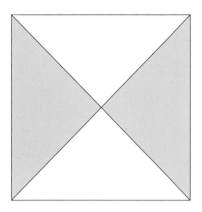

Block A

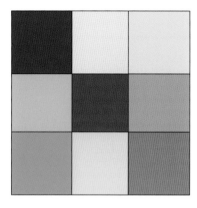

Block B

Cutting

From white fabric, cut:
(4) 10½" x WOF strips
    subcut into (16) 10½" squares
From gray fabric, cut:
(4) 10½" x WOF strips
    subcut into (16) 10½" squares
From each of 24 assorted prints, cut:
(1) 3½" x WOF strip
From binding fabric, cut:
(9) 2½" x WOF strips

> **This quilt is composed of two types of blocks: quarter-square triangle (Block A) and 9-patch (Block B). There are 32 of each block.**

Constructing the Blocks

Block A

1. Draw a diagonal line on the wrong side of each white square. **(fig. 1)**

2. Align each white square with a gray square, right sides together, and pin along the drawn line. Stitch ¼" seam on either side of the drawn line but not on the line itself. **(fig. 2)**

3. Cut units in half on the drawn line, then press seam toward the gray. Repeat for the remaining 15 pairs to create a total of 32 half-square triangles (HSTs). **(fig. 3)**

4. Pair two HSTs, right sides together, so that like colors are opposite one another **(fig. 4)**. Draw a diagonal line, perpendicular to the seams on the wrong side of one unit. Take care that the seams are "nested" and pinned at the center, as described on page 20 of A Patchwork Primer. **(fig. 5)**

5. Stitch ¼" seam on both sides of the drawn line, then cut the units in half on the drawn line. Press your seams. Repeat for the remaining 31 pairs to create a total of 32 quarter-square triangles **(fig. 6)**. Trim each

Block A to 9½", taking care to keep the seams centered at each of the corners as you trim.

⌐ PIECING TIP

Stitching these seams with the top seam facing toward the presser foot will help keep the center seams aligned more closely, since the presser foot will slightly push the seam allowances toward one another as you stitch.

- - - - - - - - - - - - - - - - - - - -

⌐ TRIMMING TIP

For an easy, accurate trimming process, invest in a 9½" square ruler. Align the center marking on the ruler with your seam intersection, and utilize the 90-degree-angle marking along one of the seams to be sure your placement is spot on. Then just trim around all four sides — nothing could be easier!

- - - - - - - - - - - - - - - - - - - -

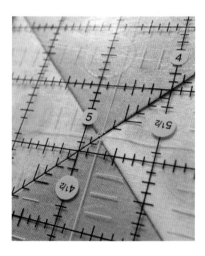

Block B

6. Sort the 3½" strips of print fabric into 8 groups of 3. Stitch the 3 strips in each group together along the length of the strip. Press seams toward one side (it doesn't matter which).

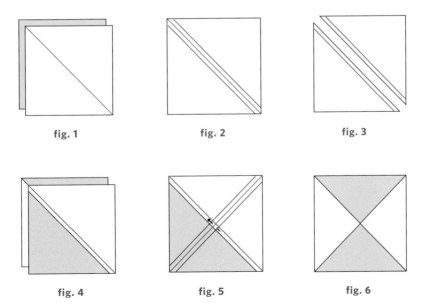

fig. 1   fig. 2   fig. 3

fig. 4   fig. 5   fig. 6

7. At one end, trim the selvage then subcut the strip set into 3½" units. Repeat for the remaining strip sets to create a total of 96 units. **(fig. 7)**

8. To create each Block B, stitch 3 units together, pinning at seam intersections. When possible, arrange units so that intersecting seams are facing opposite directions to aid in alignment and to reduce bulk. Repeat to create a total of 32 blocks.

Assembling the Quilt

9. Stitch 8 rows of 8 alternating blocks each **(fig. 8)**. Pin at each seam intersection and press all seams toward Block A. Stitch rows together and press seams to the side.

⌇ TIP
Speed this process up by employing some chain piecing! Stitch your blocks into pairs first, then the pairs into fours, and the fours into eights.

Finishing

10. Using the methods described in A Patchwork Primer beginning on page 27, piece the backing, make the quilt sandwich, pin-baste, quilt as desired, and bind.

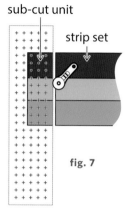

sub-cut unit

strip set

fig. 7

fig. 8

around the perimeter, leaving a 3" opening in the center of one of the sides **(fig. 9)**. Be sure to secure the beginning and end of these seams.

3. Turn right sides out; fill each beanbag with 1 cup (240 ml) dry beans and whipstitch the opening closed. Tuft the center by stitching on a large button using heavy-duty thread or embroidery floss.

⌐ TIP

This is a perfect project for involving children, giving your game night quilt even more meaning. Let little ones play with the beans, counting and sorting them, grabbing fistfuls and pouring them from cup to cup. When playtime is over, help them measure and fill the bags before you stitch them up. They'll feel such a sense of achievement every time you pull out the game quilt that they had a real hand in making.

⌐ GOOD TO KNOW

Create a more durable corner by leaving the seam allowance intact rather than clipping it. Place your index finger in a corner while the beanbag is still right sides together. Fold the seam allowance over to one side, and then fold the other seam allowance over to the same side, creating a "hospital corner". Holding the folds securely between the index finger and thumb, turn the corner right sides out. Repeat for all four corners

"Hospital Corner".

Game On: Making Beanbag Checkers Game Pieces

For a proper game of checkers, you will need 24 beanbags: 12 each of two distinct colors. Each color may contain as few or as many different prints as you like. I made each of my beanbags with two coordinating prints from the same color group.

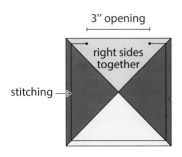

3" opening

right sides together

stitching →

fig. 9

Materials

¼ yard each of 2-4 prints, half in one color group and half in another distinct color group

(24) 1" buttons

8 lbs (128 oz /24 cups) dry beans or lentils

Heavy-duty thread or embroidery floss

Cutting

From each color group, cut:
(12) 6" squares (beanbag fronts)

(12) 5" squares (beanbag backs)

Construction

1. Pair like-colored 6" squares, right sides together, and construct 24 quarter-square triangles (Figures 1-6 page 79). Press and trim to 5" square.

2. Pair each quarter-square triangle with a same-colored 5" square, right sides together, and stitch ¼" seam

"You can discover more about a person in an hour of play
than in a year of conversation." — Plato

HIDEAWAY

Pieced by Amy Gibson, quilted by Susan Santistevan

When was the last time you played in the dirt? When was the last time you sunk both of your hands into cool, wet mud? I don't think my kids are any happier than when they're stomping in puddles, chasing bugs, spinning themselves dizzy, or laughing at their own jokes... just kids being kids. Somewhere along the road we lose this innocent fun, this wide-eyed wonder. We wake up one day to find the pinwheels have faded, and suddenly we're busy doing our taxes, calculating saturated fat, and standing in line at the post office. Well, I don't know about you, but I could use a little less of the post office lines and a little more of the puddle stomping.

That's why this quilt is about taking back our playtime. It's about getting down on our hands and knees with our kids, and letting ourselves be young again. Make a teepee. Build a fort. Play dress up. Do a puppet show. Have a tea party. Laugh, giggle, roar, growl. Allow life's simplest pleasures to tickle you silly, as you make precious memories with the little ones in your life.

Finished Quilt Size: 72" x 84"

Finished Block Size: 12" x 12"

Materials

Yardage requirements are based on 42"-wide fabric

2 yards background fabric

1⅛ yards low-volume neutral print(s), for small pinwheel frame

¼ yard each of 21 colored prints

5¼ yards backing fabric

⅝ yard binding fabric

78" x 90" batting

⌐ LOW-VOLUME PRINTS
Low-volume fabrics are print fabrics that show up as light solids (or nearly solids) in black and white photographs. These fabrics have small-scale design elements that range from geometrics to florals and other designs like text or dots. The background color can be white, cream, beige, gray, or other neutral and may include small bits of black or other colors. As long as the overall fabric appears to be a white or light solid from a distance or in a black and white photo, it can be considered a low-volume print. Incorporating low-volume printed fabrics in place of white or light solids is an excellent way to add more personality to your quilts!

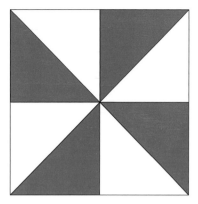

Block A

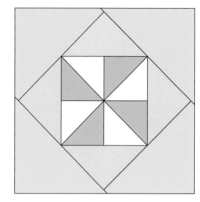

Block B

Cutting

From each of the 21 colored prints, cut:

(2) 7" squares

(2) 6⅞" squares

    subcut in half diagonally

(2) 4" squares

From background, cut:

(7) 7" x WOF strips

    subcut into (42) 7" squares

(5) 4" x WOF strips

    subcut into (42) 4" squares

From low-volume neutral, cut:

(5) 7¼" x WOF strips

    subcut into (21) 7¼" squares

    subcut into quarters by
    cutting along both diagonals

From binding fabric, cut:

(8) 2½" x WOF strips

> **This quilt is composed of 2 different blocks: large pinwheels (Block A) and smaller framed pinwheels (Block B). There are 21 of each block.**

Constructing the Blocks

Block A

1. Draw a diagonal line, on the wrong side of each 7" background square. Pair each 7" background square with a 7" colored print square, right sides together, with the drawn line facing up. Pin. You will have 42 pairs. **(fig. 1)**

2. Stitch a ¼" seam on either side of the drawn line, **(fig. 2)**. Cut each unit in half on the drawn line, then press toward the print fabric.

✂ PIECING TIP

This is a perfect time to employ some good old "mass production" to help speed things along. See the One-Woman Factory (page 36) for helpful tips on chain piecing as well as high-volume cutting and pressing.

- - - - - - - - - - - - - - - - - - -

3. Trim each HST unit to 6½" square. You will have 84 units.

✂ TRIMMING TIP

To make sure your half-square triangle unit is centered as you trim, align the 45-degree marking of your square ruler precisely on the diagonal seam.

- - - - - - - - - - - - - - - - - - -

4. Using four HST units from the same print, lay out a pinwheel using the Block A illustration as a guide. Stitch 2 rows of 2 units each. Press seams toward the print fabric. Stitch the rows together, taking care to align and pin at the center seam intersection. Press the seam toward either side. **(fig. 4)**

5. Repeat to create 21 Block A pinwheels, taking care that all the pinwheels are spinning in the same direction. Square blocks to 12½" and set aside.

Block B

6. Using the 4" colored print squares and 4" background squares, refer to Step 1 from Block A to create 84 smaller half-square triangle units. Trim these units to 3½" square.

7. Referring to Steps 4–5, stitch and press to create all 21 smaller pinwheel blocks, again taking care that all pinwheels are spinning in the same direction.

8. To add the first frame, fold a low-volume print triangle in half, and mark the center of the longest side by finger pressing. Handle triangles with care, so the raw bias edges don't stretch or distort. Align the center marking of the triangle with the center seam of a Block B, pin and stitch. Repeat with a second triangle on the opposite side of the Block B. Note that the outside corners of the triangles (dog ears) will hang off each side of the pinwheel and the triangles will overlap in the middle **(fig. 4)**. Press seams toward the triangles.

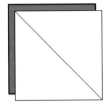

fig. 1

fig. 2

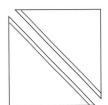

fig. 3

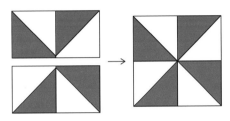

fig. 4

9. Referring to Step 8, add triangles to the remaining two sides by aligning the centers, pinning, stitching, and pressing toward the triangles **(fig. 5)**. Trim the excess fabric points (dog ears).

10. Repeat Steps 8–9, using the remaining colored print triangles to add the outer frame to all 21 Block B pinwheels. **(fig. 6)**

✐ **PIECING TIP**
Before stitching on the outer frames, sort all your blocks by selecting which small pinwheels will be paired with which outer print frames. This way, you can make sure that none of the same or similar prints end up paired together, which will make for a more balanced overall look.

- - - - - - - - - - - - - - - - - - -

11. You should now have a total of 21 Block A pinwheels and 21 Block B framed pinwheels. Press all the blocks and square to 12½".

Assembling the Quilt

12. Referencing Figure 7, stitch 7 rows of 6 blocks each, alternating the placement of Block A and Block B in each row. Pin at each seam intersection and press all seams toward Block A. Stitch rows together and press seams to the side.

Finishing

13. Using the methods described in A Patchwork Primer beginning on page 27, piece the backing, make the quilt sandwich, pin-baste, quilt as desired, and bind.

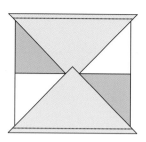

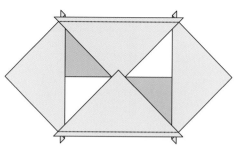

fig. 5   fig. 6

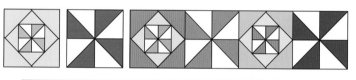

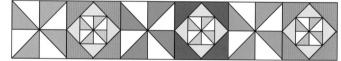

fig. 7

meaning
in the making

Every once in a while, our kids need us to be wildly enthusiastic, to meet them at their level, to shout a sunny yes in a world raining with no. In our home, quilts play a role in this effort. They make the best tents, the best puppet show stages, the best tea party tablecloths, and the best parachutes. In our home, we don't hide them away — they are scattered about the house for easy access, laundered often, enjoyed always.

SUNDAY IN THE PARK

Pieced and quilted by Amy Gibson

In our family, traditions range from fluffy Thanksgiving pumpkin chiffon to taking the defeat of our favorite sports team a little too personally. But my absolute favorite tradition comes along every summer in the form of Jazz in the Park, a beloved outdoor concert series featuring an array of local jazz bands.

Every weekend, for two full months, decked in our most comfortable sundresses and linen shorts, we pack up savory snacks, fresh berries, a bottle of wine, a game of cornhole, some hula hoops, and yes, the picnic quilt, and head to the park with family and friends for an unforgettable evening. I don't know exactly what the secret ingredient is to this magic, but I do know it is precisely that: magic. Perhaps it's lounging with the sunset on our backs, being surrounded by music, dancing barefoot in the grass, or Lindy-hopping with strangers as if we're celebrating the most joyous of weddings.

As we soak in the warmth of the evening we are doing more than just enjoying music or a park. We're creating memories to last a lifetime, and, I hope, showing our children what we cherish most. Not our cell phones, not our home improvement projects or our blogs or even our quilts, but this, right here, right now, with them. May this quilt, and the intention behind it, inspire you to pack up your own picnic basket, to spread out on the grass, and to soak in some delightfully laid-back outdoor quality time with the ones you hold dear.

Finished Quilt Size: 84" x 84"

Finished Block Size: 12" x 12"

Materials

Yardage requirements are based on 42"-wide fabric

3⅓ yards background fabric

¼ yard each of 9–12 assorted prints in 4 distinct color groupings

Color 1 (light): 9–12 prints

Color 2 (light): 9–12 prints

Color 3 (medium-dark): 9–12 prints

Color 4 (medium-dark): 9–12 prints

7¾ yards backing fabric

⅝ yard binding fabric

𝐼 DESIGN TIP

The dynamic "plaid effect" of this quilt has everything to do with fabric selection, so take care in thoughtfully choosing your four colors and the array of prints that become your groupings. The plaid pattern tends to stand out most distinctly when two contrasting medium-dark colors and two contrasting light colors, all distinct from one another, are used. While the prints within each of the four color groupings may vary in shade and scale, they need to blend with one another so as to appear as a single recognizable color, which allows for the distinct diagonal lines to form across the quilt.

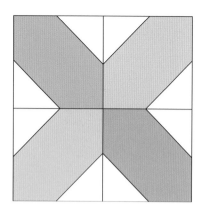

Block A

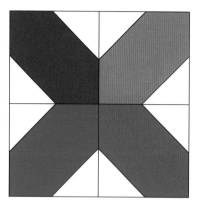

Block B

Cutting

From each Color 1 and Color 2 (light) fabric, cut:
(50) 6½" squares

From each Color 3 and Color 4 (medium-dark) fabric, cut:
(48) 6½" squares

From background fabric, cut:
(33) 3½" x WOF strips subcut into (392) 3½" squares

From binding fabric, cut:
(9) 2½" x WOF strips

> This quilt is composed of X-style blocks in 2 variations: the lighter shades (Color 1 and Color 2) and the darker shades (Color 3 and Color 4). There are 25 lighter A Blocks and 24 darker B Blocks.

Constructing the Blocks

1. Draw a diagonal line, on the wrong side of each 3½" background square.

⟁ **MARKING TIP**
Speed up this step by marking multiple squares at once, as detailed in One-Woman Factory on page 36.

2. Align two background squares in opposite corners of any color 6½" print square, right sides together, so that the drawn lines run parallel to each other **(fig. 1)**. Pin. Stitch on the drawn lines, then trim outside seam allowances to ¼" **(fig. 2)**. Press corners open. Repeat with the remaining 6½" print squares to create a total of 196 units.

3. Organize the 196 units into V-shaped pairs, combining Color 1 and Color 2, and Color 3 and Color 4. Take care that all units have consistent color placement, with Color 2 and Color 4 always on the right. Stitch pairs together, then press seams in the same direction. **(figs. 3, 4)**

4. Stitch together like units to create 25 light A blocks and 24 dark B blocks. Align and pin at the seam intersections. Press seams to the side.

Assembling the Quilt

5. Referencing Figure 5, stitch 7 rows of 7 alternating blocks each, starting with a Block A in the first spot of Row 1. Pin at each seam intersection and press all seams toward Block B. Stitch rows together and press seams to the side.

Finishing

6. Using the methods described in A Patchwork Primer beginning on page 27, piece the backing, make the quilt sandwich, pin-baste, quilt as desired, and bind.

meaning in the making

Don't let inclement weather keep you from a delightful picnic. Spread out your quilt indoors, grab a couple of comfy pillows, switch on some relaxing music, and savor a special meal with your sweeties in the comfort of your own home. Best of all, no need to pack the bug repellent!

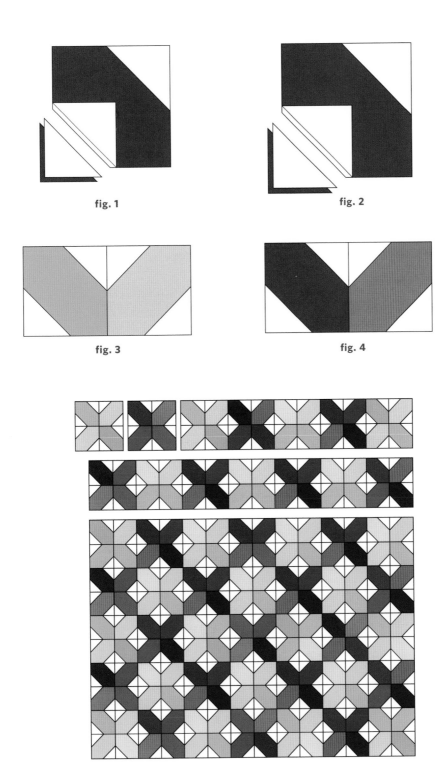

fig. 1

fig. 2

fig. 3

fig. 4

fig. 5

Carrying Strap

Make any quilt perfectly portable by stitching up this versatile carrying strap. The thick quilted construction will make toting your quilt comfortable and convenient, wherever your picnicking may take you.

All you need is 1⅛ yards of fabric and a 6"-wide strip of batting at least 120" long.

𝘍 GOOD TO KNOW

Batting can be pieced together when needed. Butt two pieces up against each other and hand stitch with some large zigzag basting stitches to hold them together. Once quilted, you'll never even know it was pieced.

Construction

1. For the main strap, cut (3) 12" x WOF strips. Trim off the selvages, then join the strips end to end, creating a single long strip. Press one short end of the fabric over ½", wrong sides together. Press the strip in half lengthwise, wrong sides together (just like a binding), then open it back up and press both long edges to meet in the center, using the crease as a guide,

along the entire length of the strip. Insert the 120" x 6" strip of batting into the folds of the strap, then fold in half lengthwise, pressing and pinning along the entire length. The batting will be shorter than the fabric, and the two should be aligned at one end **(fig. 6)**. Set aside.

2. To make the ties, cut a 2" x WOF strip from the remaining yardage. Trim the selvages, then cut the strip into 4 equal lengths. Press one short end of the fabric over ¼", wrong sides together. Repeat the same folding and pressing process used on the main strap **(fig. 6)**, for each of the 4

ties, omitting the batting. Top stitch ⅛" seam along the open edge. Set aside. **(fig. 7)**

3. Working with the main strap again, trim fabric at the raw end to 1" beyond the batting. Bring the raw end around to the finished edge, taking care that the strap is not twisted, and tuck it inside the finished end, so the ends of the batting meet. Pin. Stitch several reinforcing seams across the joint to secure.

4. With the pins still in place, lay the strap out on a table or floor. Measure 15" from the center in either direction,

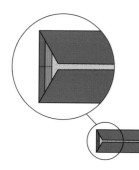

fig. 6

fig. 7

and insert the raw end of each of the 4 ties into the open edge of the strap. Pin. Using a walking foot, stitch ⅛" seam around the length of the entire strap to close the open edge and also to secure the ties in place. Continue quilting ¼" seams across the remaining width, starting at the reinforced seam and backstitching at the beginning and the end of each seam. (fig. 8)

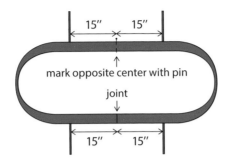

15"   15"

mark opposite center with pin

joint

15"   15"

fig. 8

Fold 'n' Go

To fold the Sunday in the Park quilt so that it fits neatly in the strap, fold the quilt into fourths, then in half again, and then into thirds. Fold over the strap and join the two ties into a bow to secure.

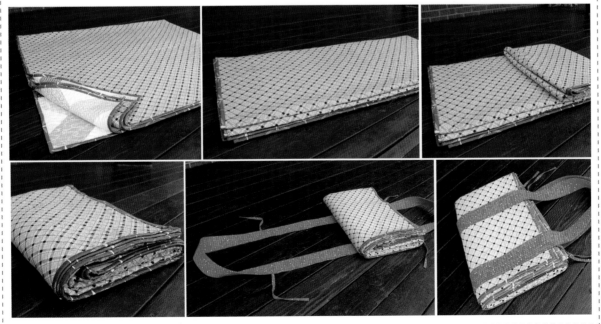

"What I make with my hands, I give of my heart." —anonymous

JAM-PACKED

My days are jam-packed around here! We are busy bees, rushing here and there, in and out, hopping from one flower to the next — work, school, church, sports, clubs, volunteering, parties, friends. Sometimes we're so focused on getting to the next place, trying to beat rush-hour traffic or cleaning the house, that we can lose sight of the little moments, the sweet reminders. The simple "You're on my mind" or "I'm so proud of you" can get lost in the mix. Intentionally seeking out those moments to share your heart, and seizing them at every possible opportunity, can make all the difference in ensuring that those around you feel extra loved. That's what this sweet little pocket lunch sack is for me — one more chance to squeeze a "You rock, kid" into their day, with happy fabrics and a special note. It's a usable, everyday gift for my fancy little ladies and my mischievous little gents, to bring a bit of fun and excitement to peanut butter and banana on whole wheat.

Finished Size, Handbag Style: base 5" x 5", height 13"

Finished Size, Hobo Style: base 5" x 5", height 8"

Materials

Yardage requirements are based on 42"-wide fabric

⅓ yard exterior fabric, quilting cotton or home dec weight

⅓ yard lining fabric

1 package Insul-Bright insulated lining (at least 36" x 10½", or 18" x 21")

Scraps for the pocket

Scrap of Pellon Shapeflex single-sided fusible interfacing (at least 3" x 1½")

¾" magnetic snap

1" button for handbag version

ᴵ GOOD TO KNOW

Although this bag is machine washable, sometimes it's nice to be able to quickly cut the grime with a wipe. Try using a fabric such as laminated cotton, vinyl, or oilcloth for your lining.

- - - - - - - - - - - - - - - - - -

Cutting

From each of the exterior fabric, lining fabrics, and Insul-Bright, cut:

(2) 10½" x 18" rectangles

From fabric scraps, cut:

(1) 2"–3" patch for the pocket center

4 or more strips of varying lengths at least 3", and 1"–2" wide

From interfacing scrap, cut:

(2) 1½" squares

Construction

1. Copy the Jam-Packed Cutting Template (see page 99). Referring to Figure 1 and the instructions on the template, make the curved cut on the top edge of the exterior, lining, and Insul-Bright pieces.

Improv Pocket

The pocket for this project is constructed using an improvisational log cabin piecing technique. Since the size of each individual fussy cut center patch is unique, every pocket will likely turn out with slightly different dimensions. This is the nature of improvisational piecing, so I encourage you to use the freedom that this technique offers to make a uniquely pieced pocket.

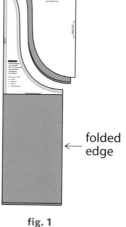

← folded edge

fig. 1

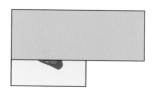

fig. 2

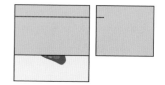

fig. 3

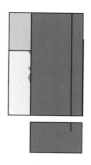

fig. 4

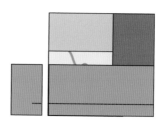

fig. 5

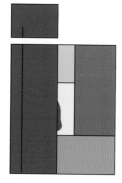

fig. 6

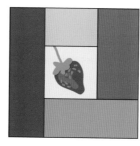

fig. 7

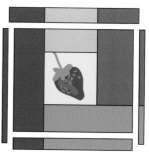

fig. 8

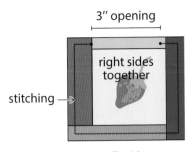

fig. 9

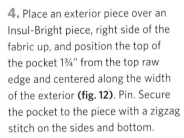

3" opening

right sides together

stitching →

fig. 10

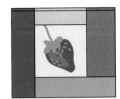

fig. 11

2. To create the log cabin style design of the pocket, start with your center scrap patch. Referencing Figure 2, stitch a strip to the right edge of the center patch, trim, then continue adding strips, working in a clockwise direction until a suitable size and look is reached, no more than 5" in either direction. Trim the pieced block to the desired size, including a ¼" seam allowance on all sides. **(figs. 2-8)**

3. For the pocket lining, cut a piece the same size as the pocket front **(fig. 9)**. Place the pocket and the pocket lining right sides together, then stitch around the exterior with a ¼" seam allowance, leaving a 3" hole at the top for turning **(fig. 10)**. Turn the piece right sides out using the technique shown on page 81 of the Make Your Move game pieces to create a sharp corner. Press the raw edges of the opening in, then topstitch a ⅛" seam along the top edge. **(fig. 11)**

4. Place an exterior piece over an Insul-Bright piece, right side of the fabric up, and position the top of the pocket 1¾" from the top raw edge and centered along the width of the exterior **(fig. 12)**. Pin. Secure the pocket to the piece with a zigzag stitch on the sides and bottom.

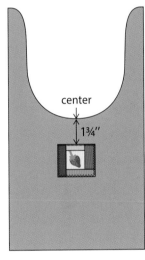

center

1¾"

fig. 12

meaning **in the making**

Lunch box notes seem to be experiencing a new surge of popularity in recent years. Try searching the web for creative new ideas. Some sites offer printable designs for really cute, funny, or clever notes. What about including a riddle, joke, or a Scripture verse? Or how about a recollection of a fun memory? Offer your loved ones encouragement, a good laugh, or just a sweet reminder that they're on your mind.

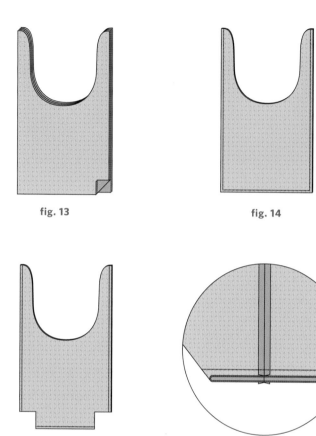

fig. 13

fig. 14

fig. 15

fig. 16

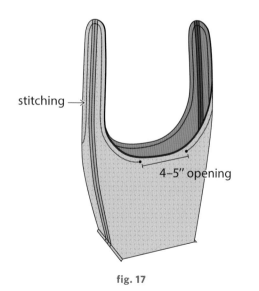

stitching →

4–5" opening

fig. 17

5. Follow the manufacturer's instructions to install the magnetic snap. Position the top of the snap 1¼" from the top raw edge of each lining piece and fuse the 1½" squares of woven interfacing behind the snaps on the wrong side of the lining.

6. Layer the exterior pieces and Insul-Bright pieces right sides together **(fig. 13)** and stitch down both sides and across the bottom. Repeat for the lining pieces. **(fig. 14)**

7. To create the box corners at the bottom of the bag, cut 2½" squares from the bottom interior and exterior pieces **(fig. 15)**. Then pull the layers open, matching the side seam with the bottom seam. Pin and stitch across both corners of each of the two pieces. **(fig. 16)**

8. Turn the lining piece right side out and place it inside the exterior piece. Pin the raw edges together **(fig. 17)** and stitch all the way around, leaving a 4"- 5" opening.

9. Pull the lining out of the exterior and turn the entire bag right side out. Then push the lining back down into the exterior of the bag. Press the top seam flat, folding in and pinning the raw edges of the opening. Topstitch ⅛" around the top of the bag.

10. For the handbag version of the lunch sack, overlap the tips of the handles by 2", then hand stitch a button on the top.

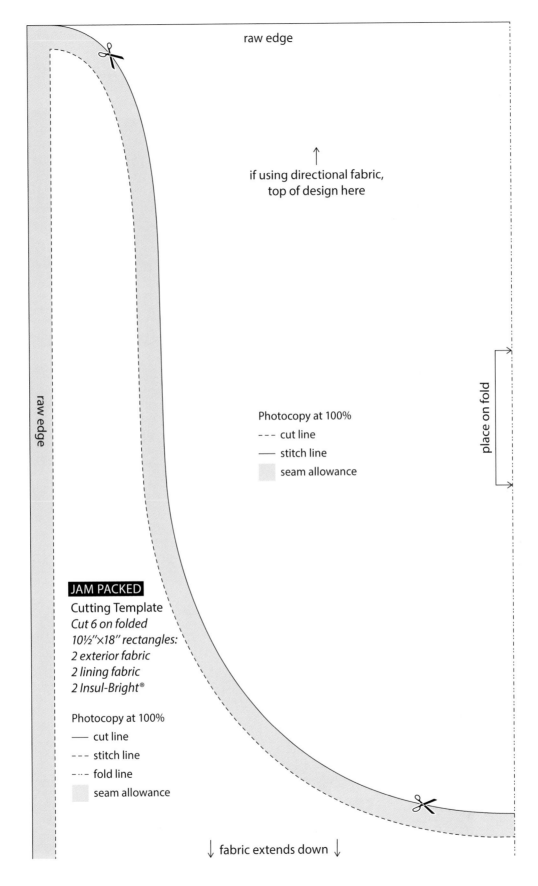

raw edge

↑

if using directional fabric,
top of design here

raw edge

place on fold

Photocopy at 100%
- - - cut line
—— stitch line
seam allowance

JAM PACKED

Cutting Template
*Cut 6 on folded
10½"×18" rectangles:
2 exterior fabric
2 lining fabric
2 Insul-Bright®*

Photocopy at 100%
—— cut line
- - - stitch line
-··- fold line
seam allowance

↓ fabric extends down ↓

"We do not remember days. We remember moments." —anonymous

MEMORY KEEPERS

Quilts are not only a wonderful way to write stories; they're also great at preserving them. The projects in this section are intended to help preserve memories of times gone by — to honor those things that are worthy of honor, and to help bring these stories to life in a practical and beautiful way. Once a story, an intention, or a tradition is captured in fabric, it ceases to be a dusty, forgotten relic in the attic, and becomes a remembered and thoroughly enjoyable part of our everyday lives. From family recipes and house numbers to special photos and meaningful letters, these projects remind us of the people and places we cherish most.

THERE'S ONLY ONE YOU

Pieced by Amy Gibson, quilted by Amy Wade

I love old family trees: neatly penciled names on a tissue-thin paper at the back of a Bible, mounted into a frame, or folded up in a drawer. This is our tribe, our clan, our kinfolk. It's an ancestry, a lineage, a road map of where we came from and perhaps where we're going. In a way, this quilt is a family tree, but it's probably different than any you've seen before. This tree doesn't have branches, it doesn't have a trunk, it doesn't tell us who Great Uncle John's second son was. But it is about our relationships to one another, about the root system that grounds us, holding fast to the soil and empowering us to stand upright.

It starts with one special person, one unique, precious little soul, blossoming in the center. And that special someone is surrounded by people who love him, by layer upon layer of love, support, and faith. These advocates — family, friends, a caring teacher, a guiding pastor, a mentor — they link arms around that fragile little acorn and water him, beckon him to grow, to sprout up strong and tall. And what happens when that little acorn is nourished and supported? He grows, yes, and suddenly is making waves of his own that ripple out into the world and provide water themselves.

May this quilt be a reminder to your little sprout that he is so very special, that he is surrounded by unfathomable love, and may it also remind you to keep on watering him, to hold fast when storms threaten to blow you both over, because one day, probably sooner than you think, he will be a great oak.

Finished Quilt Size: 60" x 72"

Finished Block Size: 6" x 6"

Materials

Yardage requirements are based on 42"-wide fabric

3¾ yards background fabric

¼ yard each of Prints A, H, I, J, K, L

½ yard each of Prints B, C, D, F, G

¾ yard of Print E

3½ yards 17"-wide double-sided fusible web (see page 14)

4¼ yards backing fabric

½ yard binding fabric

66" x 78" batting

Cutting

From background fabric, cut:

(20) 6½" x WOF strips
  subcut into (120) 6½" squares

From Prints A—L, cut:

(1) 8½" x WOF strip each for
  Prints A, I, J, K and L

(2) 8½" x WOF strips each from
  Prints B, C, D, F, G and H

(3) 8½" x WOF strips from Print E

From binding fabric, cut:

(7) 2½" x WOF strips

I DESIGN TIP

Pay special attention to the contrast between your fabrics in this quilt, for a bold echo design that pops!

Constructing the Blocks

1. Trim the selvages from the print strips, then cut each print in half, creating two strips approximately 21" long. Following the manufacturer's instructions, fuse the following number of 21" strips, right side of fabric up, to the rough side of the fusible web, so that the edges of the strips are touching and run parallel to the 17" width of the fusible web:

★ Prints A, J, K, L: fuse 1 strip

★ Prints H, I: fuse 2 strips

★ Print B: fuse 3 strips

★ Prints C, D, E, F, G: fuse 4 strips

★ For prints E and H, cut off any excess fabric hanging off the edge of the fusible web after the previous strips have been fused, and fuse that excess to the web as well.

2. Create a template from the Petal Block Appliqué Template (see page 107). Positioning the template perpendicular to each strip, use the following chart to cut the correct number of petal shapes from each print:

3. Using the machine appliqué process (see page 22), fuse and stitch one petal to each background block, taking care to center the petal, and leaving ⅜" of background fabric at each tip. **(fig. 1)**

Assembling the Quilt

4. Referencing Figure 2, stitch 12 rows of 10 blocks each. Take care to match and pin at seam intersections. Press.

Finishing

5. Using the methods described in A Patchwork Primer beginning on page 27, piece the backing, make the quilt sandwich, baste, quilt as desired and bind.

PRINT A	**4 petals**
PRINT B	**12 petals**
PRINT C	**16 petals**
PRINT D	**16 petals**
PRINT E	**18 petals**
PRINT F	**16 petals**
PRINT G	**16 petals**
PRINT H	**9 petals**
PRINT I	**6 petals**
PRINT J	**4 petals**
PRINT K	**2 petals**
PRINT L	**1 petal**

meaning
in the making

I designed this quilt for my children. This one is for my son in particular, but for our other three children to enjoy as well. If you do choose to use my same intention, keep in mind that this quilt need not be for your child, or for any child for that matter. This quilt is a big soft hug — make it for anyone to whom you want to express love and support. Maybe it's a friend going through a hard time, maybe a parent who's living alone, or maybe it's for yourself: a beautiful reminder of your value, your uniqueness, a reminder to cherish those dear ones who lift you up, as well as to ripple that encouragement out to those around you.

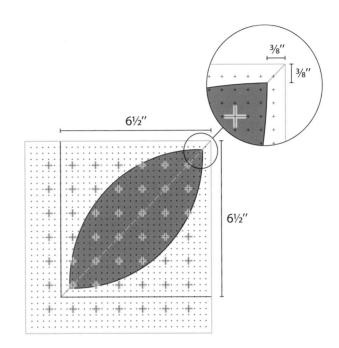

fig. 1

fig. 2

THERE'S ONLY ONE YOU

Petal Block Appliqué Template

Photocopy at 100%

"Life is like a camera. Focus on what's important and you'll capture it perfectly." — anonymous

SWEET SILHOUETTE

Pieced and framed by Amy Gibson

When it comes to meaningful patchwork, bigger isn't always better. Often the simpler, smaller pieces stand out most, and can speak our hearts in a larger way than any king-size quilt could. For me, these silhouetted portraits are just that: a timeless way for me to capture my little ones just as they are right now. To have that reminder of the sweet little shape of her nose or curve of his neck, that cute haircut we had to improvise after she took the scissors to it herself — it's priceless.

Seeing these precious reminders on my wall, day after day, surrounded by my favorite folksy shapes and little tiny patches of my most treasured scraps, many of which I've long since run out of... oh, my heart! I hope that this project brings you even just a little bit of the same joy that it does to me, and that it will remind you, as it does me, that the simple little moments in life are often the most important. Whether you stitch one up for yourself, or give one as a gift, it's sure to be a keeper.

Finished Size: 11″ x 14″

Materials

Yardage requirements are based on 42"-wide fabric

¼ yard background fabric

⅛ yard black fabric

⅛ yard medium-dark neutral fabric (I used a denim/linen blend for added texture)

38 print scraps at least 1½" square

8 print scraps at least 1½" x 3"

¼ yard Pellon Wonder-Under paper-backed fusible web

11" x 14" cotton batting

Small appliqué scissors

Craft or utility knife

Small, flat head stainless steel straight pins

White ³⁄₁₆"-thick foam core board, preferably acid-free (available at most craft and art supply stores)

11" x 14" picture frame (measurements refer to the size of the interior opening of the frame, not the exterior dimensions)

Profile photograph of your subject, preferably in digital form on a computer or tablet

Cutting

From background fabric, cut:
(1) 7½" x 10½" rectangle
(2) 7½" x 3" rectangles
(2) 10½" x 3" rectangles
(4) 3" squares

From medium neutral fabric, cut:
(4) 4" squares

From black fabric, cut:
(1) 4" x 6" rectangle

From each of the 38 small scraps, cut:
(1) 1½" square

From each of the 8 larger scraps, cut:
(1) 1½" x 3" rectangle

From fusible web, cut:
(4) 4" squares
(1) 4" x 6" rectangle

fig. 1

Construction

1. Using up all the 1½" print squares, stitch 2 rows of 9 squares each, and 2 rows of 10 squares each.

2. Using all the remaining pieces, assemble together the 5 rows **(fig. 1)**. Pin at seam intersections and press seams toward the prints.

3. To prepare the appliqué, place a 4" square of fusible web on a Sweet Silhouette Template (opposite), paper side up. Trace around it with a pencil. Using all 4 squares of fusible web, trace 2 of each of the two templates.

4. Fuse the rough side of the fusible web interfacing to the wrong side of the fabric, following the manufacturer's instructions.

5. Using small appliqué scissors, carefully cut out the shapes. Peel off the paper backing now adhered to the wrong side of the shape. Arrange the shapes in the corners of the center rectangle of the patchwork block,

leaving ¼" between the print squares and the edge of the template on both sides.

6. Fuse the pieces to the large background rectangle, following the manufacturer's instructions. Set aside.

7. Using any basic photo viewer or editor, open the profile photo of your subject on your computer or tablet. How your image appears on the screen will be a mirror image of the final silhouette. If you want the final silhouette to look exactly like your photo, flip the image horizontally on the screen. Hold your patchwork block up to the screen and resize the photo until the image fits nicely in the center of your block. Try to leave at least a 1" space on all sides for a balanced look.

8. Print the photo, then tape the printed photograph to a sunny window or light box. Layer fusible paper-backed web on top with the paper

side facing up. Using a pencil, neatly trace the subject to create a silhouette shape. Include as much or as little detail as you like, but keep in mind that you will be cutting this shape out later. At the base of the neck, simply add a smooth line to join the end points of your shape.

9. Referring to Steps 3–6, fuse the paper-backed web containing your silhouette shape to the rectangle of black fabric. Take care that you have wrong sides together, just as before. Use appliqué scissors to carefully cut around the silhouette, peel off the paper, center it on your large background rectangle, and fuse into place.

Finishing

10. Remove the backing board from your picture frame and align it in a corner of the foam core board. Trace around the two remaining sides and use a utility knife to cut out the rectangle, giving you a piece of foam core board the same size as your frame opening.

11. Lay the batting on your foam board, followed by your silhouette piece, taking care to center the block perfectly. It may take a little adjusting to get the centering just right, since the fabric will naturally cling to the batting.

12. Using your fingers to hold the layers in place, pin down the fabric along the top edge of the foam board, placing small stainless steel flat head pins about every inch. **(fig. 2)**

⫶ **GOOD TO KNOW**
It can help to use a thimble to push the pins flush with the edge of the foam board.

- -

13. In the same way, pin along the opposite edge, pulling the fabric taut but not stretched. Pin the remaining sides, working from the center out, adding pins every inch, until the entire perimeter is secured.

14. Place the piece in the frame (with the glass still in it), then fold the corners of the excess fabric flat on the back and stitch them in place with a simple whipstitch. **(fig. 3)**

⌐ GOOD TO KNOW

If a computer is not available, use a 4" x 6" photograph. Also, it is best if this photo is backlit, so try to take it in front of a sunny window or other light source. This will make your subject appear darker and will increase the contrast of light, making the silhouette easier to trace.

- - - - - - - - - - - - - - - - - -

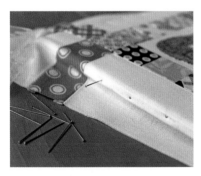

fig. 2

fig. 3

meaning **in the making**

To give this project even more meaning, consider using scraps of special clothing or linens for your focal fabrics. The little strawberry print I incorporated is especially meaningful for our family: strawberries always remind us of our grandmother, so I made strawberry dresses for all the little girls to wear to her memorial service. Sometimes it's these tiny details that make projects the most meaningful.

SWEET
SILHOUETTE
Template A
Photocopy
at 100%

SWEET
SILHOUETTE
Template B
Photocopy
at 100%

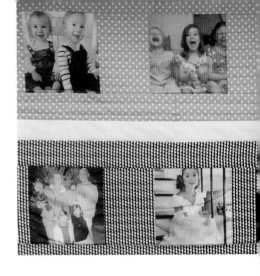

FILMSTRIP

Pieced and quilted by Amy Gibson

We live in a culture of photographs. They fill up our phones, camera cards, flash drives, and are scattered across the vast Internet galaxy like endless stars in a limitless night sky. We post them, we text them, we email them by the dozen, and then, often, they disappear into the depths of our devices. It's difficult to look back and enjoy those precious captured moments, let alone pass them down the family tree, when they're stuck in virtual space. It's important to print them out and scatter them about the home. Frame them, make them into photo books, and yes, even quilts!

That's what the Filmstrip quilt is all about: giving photos a tangible, everyday place in our homes and our lives. Because I love Instagram so much, I designed this quilt to be a perfect fit for my favorite square photos. There are loads of options for printing photos, and thanks to websites such as Spoonflower (see Resources, page 136), it's now easier than ever to print photos onto durable, high-quality fabric. This quick and easy quilt can be stitched up in an afternoon, so the real challenge isn't the sewing, but rather the choosing. Narrowing my photo picks down to just 25 was not a task for the faint of heart!

Finished Quilt Size: 50" x 56"

Materials

Yardage requirements are based on 42"-wide fabric

⅓ yard background fabric

½ yard each of 5 prints

25 photos, each measuring 6½" square, printed onto fabric (¼" on all 4 sides will be hidden in the seam allowance, so crop your photos accordingly)

3¾ yards backing fabric

½ yard binding fabric

56" x 62" batting

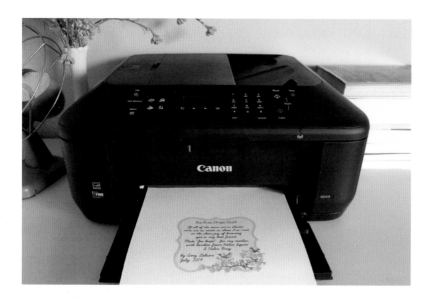

Printing Your Photos onto Fabric

Thanks to advancing technologies, there are now a wide range of options for printing your photos onto fabrics perfectly suited for sewing, washing, and pressing. These options vary in durability, printing quality, ease, convenience, and cost, so take your time in researching and deciding which technique is right for you. Before printing all your photos for this quilt, print a few test photos on a variety of substrates to test how your printer works with each product. Wash, dry, and press each test fabric, to be sure you're happy with the result of your selected method or product. Search online for ideas, tips, photo tutorials, videos, and product reviews, all of which can be very helpful.

Printing at Home

There are a variety of printable fabric products on the market that are designed to feed through a home color printer or color copy machine. I've listed a few of these products in the

Resources section (see page 136). Here are a few questions you should answer before purchasing a printable fabric product:

★ Is the product washable?
★ Can the product be pressed?
★ Is your printer suited for printing photos?
★ Is it affordable?

For this project, with photos sized to 6½" square, you can fit 1 photo per sheet of photo transfer paper, so this method would require 25 sheets. You can also easily create your own printable fabric sheets. One method involves spraying a piece of card stock paper with adhesive (make sure that the adhesive is acid-free and repositionable), then pressing it to the wrong side of background cotton fabric and trimming the fabric to the size of the card stock. Another method utilizes freezer paper instead of spray adhesive and card stock. Cut freezer paper into 8½" x 11" pieces, then press the shiny side of the paper to the wrong side of the fabric and trim to size. Both of these methods allow you to reuse the paper portion of the printable sheet.

Create your own printable fabric sheets using just a few readily available supplies.

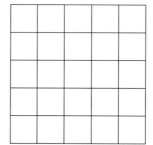

Maximize your custom fabric order by arranging your photos in a grid.

Printing Services

I enjoy the quality and ease of ordering custom printed fabric from services such as spoonflower.com. Not only do these services provide professional printing on a variety of high-quality fabric types, they also offer the option of printing larger sizes, rather than being limited to 8½" x 11" sheets.

Printing Your Filmstrip Quilt Photos on Spoonflower

The proper preparation of your photo file is an important part of ensuring that your printed images are clear and correctly sized. Start by using a photo editing program to crop and resize each photo to 975 x 975 pixels. This size will yield a 6½" x 6½" photo with a standard print quality of 150 ppi (pixels per inch). To avoid blurriness, take care to start with photos that are no smaller than this size or resolution.

To print all 25 photos onto a single yard of fabric, use a photo editing program to create a JPEG file made up of a 5 x 5 grid that contains all your photos. Since each individual photo must maintain the 975 pixel dimensions, the full size of my grid was 4875 x 4875 pixels with a resolution of 150 ppi.

Spoonflower offers an extensive array of helpful FAQs, tutorials, and instructional articles on how to prepare, test, order, and care for your fabric. Visit their site for more help.

I used Spoonflower to print my images onto fabric.

Cutting

From background fabric, cut:
(5) 2" x WOF strips

From each of the 5 colors, cut:
(1) 6½" x WOF strip
    subcut into:
        (4) 6½" x 4½" rectangles
        (2) 6½" x 2½" rectangles
        (3) 2½" x WOF strips

From photo fabric, cut:
(25) 6½" x 6½" photos

From binding fabric, cut:
(6) 2½" x WOF strips

Assembling the Quilt

1. Trim the selvages from all the WOF strips and stitch them end to end creating a long strip for each of the 5 colors plus the white (6 long strips total).

2. Assemble the quilt using Figure 1 as a guide.

3. Each strip will begin and end with a 6½" x 2½" rectangle. Arrange the rows by laying out alternating photograph squares with the corresponding colored 6½" x 4½" rectangles (remembering to end with the second 6½" x 2½" rectangle).

4. Repeat for the remaining four rows being sure to use a separate color for each row.

5. Piece the rows together and press seams away from the photograph squares.

6. Attach the corresponding WOF strip to the top and bottom of each filmstrip row pressing seams toward the WOF strips.

7. Attach a background strip to the bottom of Row 1 WOF strip and press seams away from the background strip.

8. Repeat for the next four rows being sure to eliminate the additional background strip in the last row (Row 5).

9. Piece the rows together and press the seams in one direction.

I PIECING TIP

When adding the horizontal strips, use the strip of fabric itself, smoothed on top of a pressed row of sashed photos, to determine the needed length before trimming. Since a measuring tape doesn't lay the same way that fabric does, this can be a very accurate way to measure strips.

Finishing

10. Using the methods described in A Patchwork Primer beginning on page 27, piece the backing, make the quilt sandwich, baste, quilt as desired and bind.

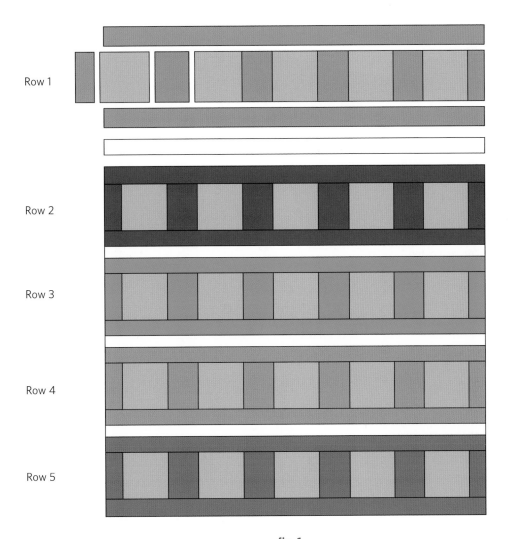

fig. 1

LOVE LETTERS

Pieced by Amy Gibson, quilted by Susan Santistevan

Not long ago, as I carefully sifted through a box of treasured family keepsakes for the very first time — amid faded newspaper clippings and stiff cardboard photographs — I came upon a series of letters, poems really, written by my great-grandmother's sister, "Nellie," in 1913. She was thirteen years old. Nellie tragically passed away at the age of sixteen, so I never knew her as I did my great-grandmother. My hands trembled as I held the delicate paper of a letter written to "Daddy," her late father, and I read it over and over, soaking in her grief, regret, and love. I was stunned to have made such an unexpected and thoroughly tangible connection with this young woman, whom I never knew.

To run my fingers over the neat rows of words and feel the imprint made by the pencil she held, to notice the way she looped her y's or the smudge in the margin that could have come from a tear that trickled down her freckled cheek or the condensation from a glass of cool water straight from the pump — I suddenly realized how very priceless and enduring these letters were. No email or text message, no status update or tweet could ever compare to the lasting beauty of this treasure: handwritten words, straight from the heart, through the hand, to the page to me. This quilt is a reminder of how very special and truly irreplaceable a handwritten letter can be. I hope it inspires you, as it does me, to slow down once in a while, to log off, pick up a pencil, and write.

Finished Quilt Size: 60" x 60"

Finished Block Size: 12" x 12"

MATERIALS

Yardage requirements are based on 42"-wide fabric

2⅝ yards background fabric

1 yard gray (any dark neutral) fabric

¾ yard handwritten/text print

¼ yard each of 25 varied prints

4 yards backing fabric

½ yard binding fabric

66" x 66" batting

Cutting

From background fabric, cut:

(3) 4½" x WOF strips
> subcut into (25) 4½" squares

(7) 5" x WOF strips
> subcut into (50) 5" squares

(10) 4½" x WOF strips
> subcut into (200) 4½" x 1⅞" rectangles

From gray fabric, cut:

(19) 1⅞" x WOF strips
> subcut into (400) 1⅞" squares

From handwritten print, cut:

(5) 4½" x WOF strips
> subcut into (100) 4½" x 1⅞" rectangles

From each of the 25 varied prints, cut:

(2) 5" squares

From binding fabric, cut:

(7) 2½" x WOF strips

Constructing the Blocks

1. Pair each 5" print square with a 5" background square and use the half-square triangles (HST) construction method (see page 79) to create 100 HSTs from the 50 pairs. Press and trim each unit to 4½" square, and set aside.

ℐ **GOOD TO KNOW**

Before marking all 400 gray squares, consider the time-saving option of stitching the diagonal lines by sight, without any markings. Practice on a couple of extra squares, and if you find that you are able to confidently stitch a straight line across these small squares, skip marking and save yourself a tedious step.

- -

2. Draw a diagonal line, on the wrong side of each gray square. Pair two gray squares with a background rectangle,

right sides together, align at the outer edges, and stitch on the lines **(fig. 1)**. Be sure the seams are perpendicular and not parallel. Trim seam allowance to ¼" **(fig. 2)** and press open **(fig. 3)**. Repeat with all gray squares and background rectangles.

ℐ **GOOD TO KNOW**

Save time during trimming by using the corner of a square ruler to trim both seams on each unit without having to reposition the ruler (fig. 4). This can be done on any size "wing" or flying geese units, as the two diagonal seams will always create a 90-degree angle.

- -

3. Referencing Figure 5, stitch a "wing" unit to either side of a print rectangle. Press seams toward the text print to create 100 "butterfly" units.

4. Referencing Figure 6, assemble 25 blocks by stitching 3 rows of 3 units each, pressing seams toward the HST blocks, pinning at seam intersections and stitching the rows together. Press and square to 12½" as needed.

Assembling the Quilt

5. Stitch 5 rows of 5 blocks each, then stitch rows together. Pin at each seam intersection and press seams open to reduce bulk. **(fig. 6)**

Finishing

6. Using the methods described in A Patchwork Primer beginning on page 27, piece the backing, make the quilt sandwich, baste, quilt as desired and bind.

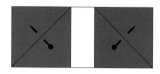

fig. 1

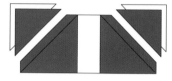

fig. 2

fig. 3

meaning in the making

With the convenience of custom fabric printing right at our fingertips, thanks to websites like Spoonflower, why not take this idea even further by creating and printing fabric from actual letters that hold deep meaning to you: the soldier who wrote to his bride during the war, the child writing mom and dad from camp — their words, their handwriting, preserved in an utterly unique and functional keepsake. See page 114 of the Filmstrip quilt for more information about printing your own fabric.

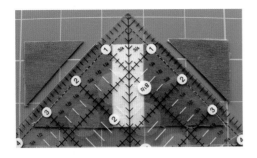

fig. 4

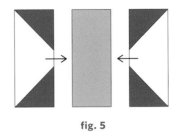

fig. 5

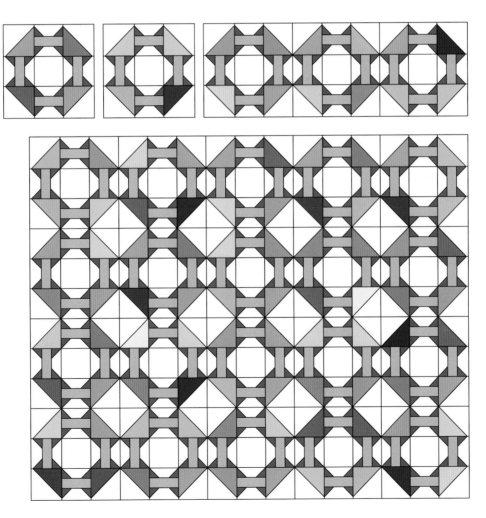

fig. 6

"If I ever go looking for my heart's desire again, I won't look any further than my own back yard. Because if it isn't there, I never really lost it to begin with." — L. Frank Baum

HOME IS WHERE THE HEART IS

Pieced and quilted by Amy Gibson

As I write this, nearly to the day, our not-so-little-anymore family has been a family for 11 years. Just more than a decade and we've had 3 pets, 4 kids, 5 jobs, and 6 homes. And it's funny, because when I really stop to think about it, somehow it's the homes that have defined periods for us. There was the "Yay, we're married; let's follow our dreams and fix up a house together!" period — our family's infancy. Then we had our first child and stumbled into the "Let's run in vast fields of beige carpet in the suburbs" period — a soft, however short-lived phase. And of course I'll never forget the "Let's sell all our stuff and move to a tiny historic apartment" period — the year of simplification and renewed priorities. Even though I know that all these homes were nothing but brick and mortar, really — just shells that we occupied for a while until it was time to move on to the next — I love that the first thing that comes to mind when I recall nearly any memory is the recollection of which home we were in. I guess it's how I keep life organized in my mind. Each move brought change; and change brought growth, renewal, fulfillment… in a nutshell, the gradual shaping of our family, one front door at a time. That's what this quilt is all about: remembering our journey and the roofs we've lived under along that journey. Some were new, some old, big, small, some for just a few months, and others that we would have loved to stay in forever — each an undeniable step toward who we are and who we will become. Where will the path lead next? I don't know, but I do know there's room in my heart for wherever it takes us.

Finished Quilt Size: 72" x 84"

Finished Block Size: 12" x 12"

MATERIALS

Yardage requirements are based on 42"-wide fabric

3¼ yards background fabric

1 yard for gray house roofs

2⅛ yards for gray houses

¼ yard each of 4 different fabrics for heart house roofs

⅞ yard for heart houses

5¼ yards backing fabric

⅝ yard binding fabric

78" x 90" batting

Cutting

From background fabric, cut:

(8) 2½" x WOF strips

(9) 6½" x WOF strips

    subcut into (84) 6½" x 4" rectangles

(9) 3⅞" x WOF strips

    subcut into (84) 3⅞" squares

From gray house roof fabric, cut:

(4) 7¼" x WOF strips

    subcut into (17) 7¼" squares

From gray house fabric, cut:

(12) 2½" x WOF strips

(5) 6½" x WOF strips

    subcut into (65) 6½" x 3" rectangles

From the 4 heart house roof fabrics, cut:

(5) total 7¼" squares

From heart house fabric, cut:

(4) 2½" x WOF strips

(2) 6½" x WOF strips

    subcut into (19) 6½" x 3" rectangles

From binding fabric, cut:

(7) 2½" x WOF strips

Constructing the Blocks

This quilt is composed of 42 blocks. There are 4 different color combinations of the block. **(figs. 1-4)**

1. The doors and side walls of the houses are constructed using strip sets.

Using all the 2½" x WOF strips, stitch the strips together along the long edges in groups of 3, creating 6 strip sets of a gray-background fabric-gray combination, and 2 strip sets of a pink-background fabric-pink combination.

2. Subcut the strip sets (see page 80) into 3½" units. You will need 65 for the gray houses, and 19 for the heart houses. Set these units aside.

3. The roofs are flying geese units. Each group of 4 geese requires (1) 7¼" square of the roof fabric and (4) 3⅞" squares of background fabric.

4. Follow the instructions on page 56 to assemble 65 flying geese for the gray roofs, and 19 for the heart roofs. There will be 7 excess geese. Each unit should measure 3½" x 6½".

5. Referencing Figure 5 and using the flying geese, the strip set units, and the solid rectangles, piece the 42 blocks in the 4 color variations. **(fig. 5)**

Assembling the Quilt

6. Stitch 7 rows of 6 blocks each, then stitch rows together. Take care to pin at each seam intersection and press all seams to the side. **(fig. 6)**

Finishing

7. Using the methods described in A Patchwork Primer beginning on page 27, piece the backing, make the quilt sandwich, baste, quilt as desired, and bind.

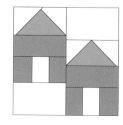

fig. 1 Color Combination 1: 30 blocks

fig. 2 Color Combination 2: 7 blocks

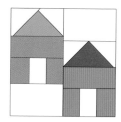

fig. 3 Color Combination 3: 3 blocks

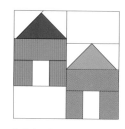

fig. 4 Color Combination 4: 2 blocks

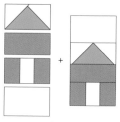

fig. 5

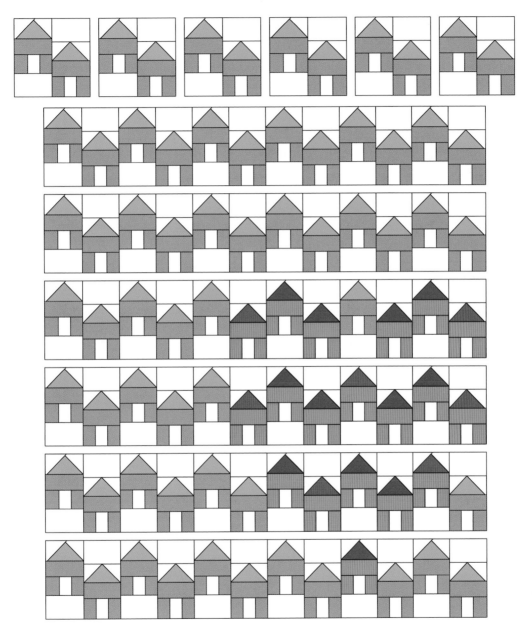

fig. 6

Within the photograph, the following recipe text is visible:

PECAN PIE

1-1/2 cups   Sugar
              Salt

CINNAMON COOKIES

1   c. sifted flour   1/2 c. sugar
1/2 t. baking powder   1   whole egg
1/8 t. salt   1   egg, sepa
                            1/2 c. chopped n

...reased pan. Sift togeth
...ts. Mix, until creamy,
... whole egg, and 1 egg yo
...iry ingredients. Spread
...kle with nuts. Bake un
...; cut into squares.
      Time: 15 to 18 min.

"Traditions. Those little rituals passed down from generation to generation that help shape your family by creating a sense of unity, warmth and closeness." — anonymous

FAMILY SECRETS

Pieced and quilted by Amy Gibson

No, no, I'm not talking about the kind of family secrets that get blurted out over the Thanksgiving table after too many glasses of merlot. It's all about food with me, as usual. Not just any food, but the most cherished, most beloved family recipes that we learned to make from our mother and she from her mother... the kind of recipes we can't imagine sending our grown children into the world without.

In our family, these cherished recipes include crepe-style Swedish pancakes made for every celebratory breakfast under the sun, a cheesy spinach soufflé brought to every holiday gathering for as long as I can remember, and pumpkin chiffon, the lightest, fluffiest Christmas dessert, which will never stop reminding me of my mother. Oh, how she loves the pumpkin chiffon. No one can toast the crunchy, nutty topping quite as meticulously as she can.

These are the recipes that I hold dear, and that I want to make sure I pass on to my children. What better way to officially pass down food traditions than to gift this little recipe-filled binder to someone at a graduation or a wedding. As they venture out into the world to make their own life, their own home, their own family, send your loved ones off with a thoughtful handmade keepsake that pays homage to family and the times spent together around the table.

Finished Size: 4" x 6", holds 3" x 5" recipe cards

Materials

Yardage requirements are based on 42"-wide fabric

Scraps from 18 prints, each at 1½" x 3"

⅛ yard for exterior "spine" fabric

¼ yard lining fabric

¼ yard pocket fabric

¼ yard fusible fleece

(1) ½"- 1" button

Perle cotton

Scrap of cotton twine

Cutting

From each of 18 different print scraps, cut:
(2) 1½" squares

From exterior "spine" fabric, cut:
(1) 6½" x 2½" rectangle

From lining fabric, cut:
(1) 6½" x 8½" rectangle

From pocket fabric, cut:
(1) 6½" x 8½" rectangle

From fusible fleece, cut:
(2) 6½" x 8½" rectangles

Construction

1. From the square scraps, stitch 6 rows of 6 squares each **(fig. 1)**. Join the rows to create 2 units, each 3 squares x 6 squares, for the exterior front and back of the binder. **(fig. 2)**

2. Stitch the scrappy units to either side of the "spine" rectangle, along the 6½" side **(fig. 3)**. This is the exterior.

3. Following the manufacturer's instruction, fuse the fleece to the wrong side of both the exterior and the lining panels. Machine and/or hand quilt the exterior as desired.

4. Fold the pocket piece in half along the 8½" side, right sides together, and stitch a ¼" seam along the 6½" raw edge, creating a tube **(fig. 4)**. Press the seam open, then turn the tube right side out and press flat so that the seam is centered at the back of the piece.

5. Topstitch a ⅛" seam on both folds of the pocket and place it on the lining, right side up. The pocket should be centered **(fig. 5)**. Stitch a seam down the center, along the length dividing the pocket in half.

6. Position the button on the right side of the exterior piece, ½" from one of the shorter ends, center and stitch into place being sure to secure it with a knot on the wrong side of the panel.

7. Place the exterior and lining panels right sides together, pin, and stitch around the perimeter, leaving a 3" opening on one of the patchwork ends opposite the edge with the button.

8. Clip the corners to reduce bulk, then turn the binder right side out and lightly press flat (be careful to follow the fleece manufacturer's

instructions for pressing, to avoid melting or shrinkage). Through the opening, push out the corners using a chopstick or similar to get nice square corners.

9. Cut a 7" length of cotton twine or string, tie a knot at the end, then positioned at the back edge of the binder opposite the button, pull it through the fold of the seam allowance. **(fig. 6)**

10. Stitch the opening closed with a blind stitch **(fig. 7)**

11. To secure the binder closed, wrap the string around the button several times.

The inside of the binder stores recipes on both sides allowing you to feature a treasured fabric for the pockets.

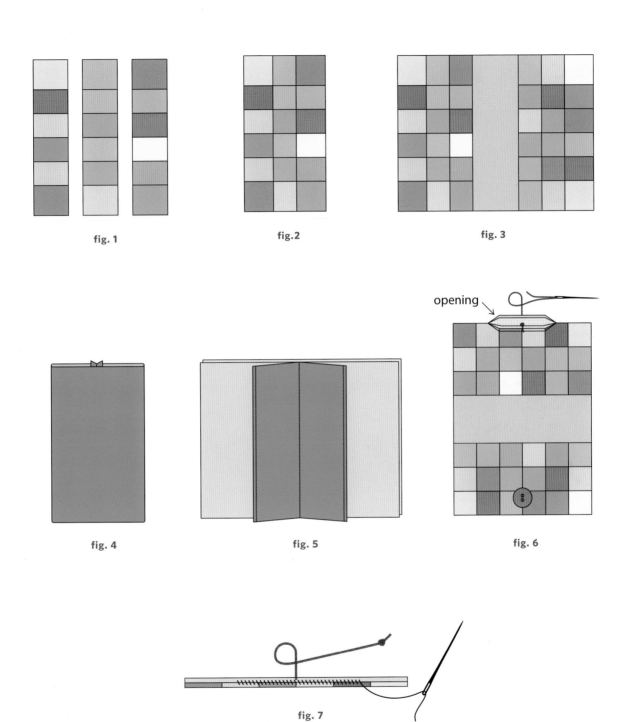

fig. 1

fig.2

fig. 3

fig. 4

fig. 5

opening

fig. 6

fig. 7

RAINDROPS

pieced by Amy Gibson, quilted by Susan Santistevan

Life can be crackling campfires, naps in a hammock, and the very best spaghetti and meatballs. It can be laughter and joy and giggles and fun — the best of memories. But sometimes, it can also be rain clouds. It can be pain and loss and tears. This quilt is about recognizing those tears, about listening and understanding. It's about just being there, and showing someone that even when their skies darken and the thunder rolls, they aren't alone in the storm.

I've incorporated vintage hankies, just a few of many given to me in cards and letters by my grandmothers throughout my childhood, partly to pay homage to these unforgettable women, but also because I am taken with the meaning behind a handkerchief. There's a reason that handkerchiefs are traditional gifts for both weddings and funerals. A hanky can dry a tear or blow a nose. It can wrap up a little treasure, or bandage a wound. A hanky can say "I recognize that you have tears, and I want to be here for you, and dry them if I can." Adorned with lush flowers, pretty scallops, or just a simple monogram, a hanky is a nostalgic symbol of compassion and kindness, and I can't think of a more heartfelt gift to give when words just aren't enough. What better way to honor their significance than to gather and highlight them in a quilt.

Finished Quilt Size: 63⅝" x 63⅝"

Finished Block Size: 15" x 15"

Materials

Yardage requirements are based on 42"-wide fabric

4½ yards background fabric

36 various scraps, each measuring at least 2" x 3½"

4 yards 17"-wide lightweight double-sided fusible web (see page 14)

9 handkerchiefs, each no larger than 14" across and preferably without a lace, crocheted, or scalloped edge

4¼ yards backing fabric

½ yard binding fabric

70" x 70" batting

Cutting

From background fabric, cut:

(2) 22½" WOF strips

> subcut each strip into (2) 22½" squares and (1) 11½" square

> cut the (2) 22½" squares into quarters along both diagonals (these will be the 8 side triangles)

> cut the 11½" square in half along one diagonal (these will be the 4 corner triangles)

(1) 15½" square

(6) 15½" x WOF strips

> subcut into (12) 15½" squares (including the cut above, you will have (13) 15½" squares)

From binding fabric, cut:

(7) 2½" x WOF strips

Constructing the Blocks

1. Following the manufacturer's instructions, fuse the wrong side of the 9 handkerchiefs to the rough side of the fusible web. Cut out the hankies, squaring them as you cut. The cut sizes can vary, as long as none is larger than 14" across. Set aside.

2. Fuse the 36 scraps to the remaining fusible web.

⌐ GOOD TO KNOW

To avoid wrinkles when fusing, steam press and starch the hankies before fusing the web. If your hanky is especially delicate or contains an embellishment, lower the temperature of the iron and press from the back first, then spot press the front, avoiding raised areas to prevent scorching. First trim off any rolled or finished edge that could prevent the square from laying flat. If your hanky has gorgeous edging consider selecting a different hanky option for this quilt.

3. Create a cardboard or plastic template from the Raindrop Template (see page 134), then cut out a total of 36 raindrop shapes from the fused scraps. Set aside.

4. Using the machine appliqué steps detailed on page 22 of A Patchwork Primer, fuse and stitch each hanky to a 15½" background block, taking care to center the design. Set aside.

⌐ GOOD TO KNOW

Find and mark a center line of any block by folding it in half and pressing. To find the center of a square block, fold it into fourths, then press. Unfold the square; the center is where the pressed lines cross.

5. Peel the paper backing off all the raindrop shapes. Referencing Figures 1-3, position, fuse, and stitch them to the remaining background squares and triangles. Each remaining square should have four drops that touch points in the center of the block **(fig. 1)**, while the larger triangles have two drops **(fig. 2)** and the smallest triangles have just one drop **(fig. 3)**. Attach appliqués at least ⅜" from the outside edge onto the triangle blocks to create the perimeter of the quilt.

⌐ TIP

Take care when handling triangle-shaped blocks because the biased edges can be easily stretched and distorted. Use of spray starch when pressing these blocks can also help minimize any potential distortion.

Assembling the Quilt

6. Stitch the blocks into 5 rows, adding the side triangles at the ends of rows. Sew rows 1–3 together, rows 4–5 together, and then stitch the two sections together for the quilt top. Finally, add the corner triangles at the corners of the quilt **(fig. 4)**. When stitching a square with a side triangle, align the right angles rather than the point. Also, when adding the corner triangles, align blocks at center lines (points will extend off the edges). Take care to pin at each seam intersection and press.

Finishing

7. Using the methods described in A Patchwork Primer beginning on page 27, piece the backing, make the quilt sandwich, baste, quilt as desired, and bind.

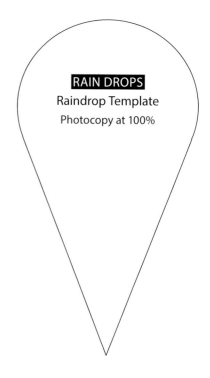

RAIN DROPS
Raindrop Template
Photocopy at 100%

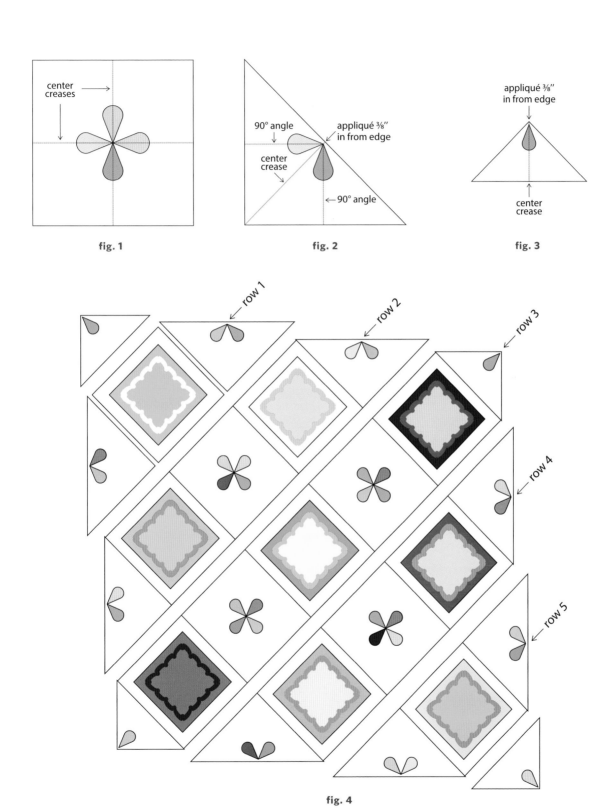

center
creases

fig. 1

90° angle

center
crease

appliqué ⅜″
in from edge

← 90° angle

fig. 2

appliqué ⅜″
in from edge

center
crease

fig. 3

row 1

row 2

row 3

row 4

row 5

fig. 4

the Rain Drops Quilt

Of all of the tears we've shared,
none are as sweet as those I've cried
in the sheer joy of knowing
you're my best friend.
Made "for keeps", for my mother,
with hankies from Helen Squire
& Helen Burg

by Amy Gibson
July, 2014

meaning
in the making

If you're gifting your quilt, handwrite a personal letter or card to accompany it explaining your intention behind it. Better yet, incorporate this intention into a permanent quilt label. The Internet offers many ideas and tutorials for creating quilt labels. My favorite way is to design them on my computer, print onto fabric, then appliqué to the back of my quilt. See page 114 of the Filmstrip quilt for more information about printing onto fabric.

HAIL THE HANKIE

Vintage handkerchiefs, in their endless array of colors and designs, are little treasures-- each holds a precious piece of history. They are utterly collectible, and a fabulous resource for use in all kinds of sewing, crafting, and home decor projects. From happy party buntings to elegant quilt blocks, projects that utilize these little gems are packed with sentimentality and nostalgia.

If you don't already have a growing collection, it's easy to start one! Keep your eyes peeled at estate and yard sales, flea markets, antique shops, vintage consignment shops, and thrift stores. Ebay and Etsy are also packed with vintage hankies, but do take care to read the product descriptions carefully as some sellers offer fabric squares printed to look like vintage hankies, that are in fact brand new-- still a fun material to work with, no doubt, but unfortunately lacking the history of a true vintage handkerchief.

Washing hankies need not be a daunting task. Keep it simple by considering how they would have been cared for when they were first made, before the arrival of washing machines and electric driers. To gently clean and freshen my hankies, I hand wash them in mild, dye/perfume-free detergent, and avoid scrubbing, followed by a thorough rinse, and a line dry. A couple of days out in the warm sunshine brightens colors and reduces stains.

For a more intensive, stain-removing wash, add 1 cup of baking soda and 1 teaspoon of cream of tartar (found with the spices, also known as potassium bitartrate). Boil hankies for 30 minutes, then rinse with cold water, followed by a basic hand wash and line dry as described above. A word of caution- if your hankies are particularly thin and worn, the boiling wash could cause damage, so consider a simple cold wash for these instead. Also take care with very saturated reds, as the heat will increase the risk of color bleeding.

Most importantly, enjoy these sweet lovelies, and have fun incorporating them into your meaningful, everyday patchwork!

RESOURCES

BOOKS

Alison Glass Appliqué: The Essential Guide to Modern Appliqué, by Alison Glass

Playful Little Paper-Pieced Projects: 37 Graphic Designs and Tips from Top Modern Quilters, by Tacha Bruecher

Free-Motion Quilting with Angela Walters: Choose and Use Quilting Designs on Modern Quilts, by Angela Walters

Lucky Spool's Essential Guide to Modern Quilt Making, compiled by Susanne Woods

Heirloom Machine Quilting: A Comprehensive Guide to Hand-Quilting Effects Using Your Sewing Machine, by Harriet Hargrave

Mastering Machine Appliqué: The Complete Guide Including: Invisible Machine Appliqué, Satin Stitch, Blanket Stitch and Much More, by Harriet Hargrave

SUPPLIES

English Paper Piecing Templates: www.paperpieces.com

Glue Basting Tips html: http://purpledaisiesquilting.com

Fabric Printing: www.spoonflower.com

Sewing Table Tutorial: www.frommartawithlove.com

REFERENCES

Baum, L. Frank. The Wonderful Wizard of Oz. Eltanin Publishing, 2013. Electronic Edition.

Chapman, Gary, and Jocelyn Green. The 5 Love Languages: Military Edition. Chicago: Northfield Publishing, 2013. Print.

Finley, Janet. Quilts in Everyday Life, 1855-1955: A 100-Year Photographic History. Altgen, PA: Schiffer Publishing, Ltd., 2012. Print.

Fisher, M.K. As They Were. New York: Vintage Books, 1983. Print.

Hemingway, Ernest. Retrieved from http://izquotes.com/quote/344114.

Jefferson, Thomas. The Writings of Thomas Jefferson, vol. XV. Bergh, Albert, ed. Retrieved from http://www.constitution.org/tj/jeff15.txt.

Precourt, Stephanie. "I Think I Wrote This to Myself." Adventures in Babywearing blog. November 24, 2008. Accessed May-July, 2014.

Reagan, Nancy. I Love You, Ronnie: The Letters of Ronald Reagan to Nancy Reagan. New York: Random House, 2002. Print.

Sach, Jacky. The Little Giant Encyclopedia: Tea Leaf Reading. C.S. Lewis. New York: Sterling, 2008. Print.

Stoval, Dee Dee. Picnic: 125 Recipes with 29 Seasonal Menus. North Adams, MA: Storey Publishing, 2001. Print.

Welty, Eudora. One Writer's Beginnings: Eudora Welty. New York: Warner Books, 1985. Print.

Whittaker, Carlos. Moment Maker: You Can Live Your Life or It Will Live You. Grand Rapids, MI: Zondervan, 2013. Audiobook.